DANIEL WEBSTER
Defender of the Union

It was big news. A store was opening in Salisbury. Daniel and his sisters walked to town almost every day that first week just to smell pickles and peppers in open barrels and stare at hard horehound candy in a glass jar on the shelf behind the counter.

But it wasn't horehounds that Daniel bought with his first pennies. It was a cotton handkerchief decorated with flags and printed on both sides—with the new Constitution of the United States of America.

Daniel's father had gone to the New Hampshire convention. He helped the ninth state to ratify the Constitution and thus to create the United States of America. Daniel showed his handkerchief to everyone but lent it to no one, not even for long enough to wash it. He read it over and over again, and its words influenced him all the rest of his life.

The farm boy who loved books became lawyer, congressman, senator, Secretary of State. In the halls of Congress he debated Henry Clay and John C. Calhoun. Before the Supreme Court he argued for freedom from government intrusion for little Dartmouth College. Through every turn in his career, the silver-tongued orator was found always on the same side of every political debate—the side of the United States of America.

Daniel Webster

Defender of the Union

by

Robert Allen

illustrated by **Michael L. Denman**

MOTT MEDIA

COPYRIGHT © 1989 by Mott Media, Inc.

Kurt Dietsch, Cover Artist

LIBRARY OF CONGRESS CATALOGING IN PUBLICATION DATA

Allen, Robert A.
      Daniel Webster: Defender of the Union / by Robert Allen; illustrated by Michael L. Denman.

      p.   cm. — (Sowers series)
      Bibliography: p. 163
      Includes index.

      SUMMARY: Traces the life of the orator and statesman who served as congressman, senator, and Secretary of State and supported the Compromise of 1850 in hopes of saving the Union. ISBN 0-88062-156-7
      1. Webster, Daniel, 1782-1852—Juvenile literature.
2. Legislators—United STates—Biography—Juvenile literature.
3. United States. Congress. Senate—Biography—Juvenile literature. 4. United States—Politics and government—1815-1861-Juvenile literature. [1. Webster, Daniel, 1782-1852.
2. Statesmen.]   I. Denman, Michael L., ill. II. Title.
III. Series: Sowers.
E340,W4A79   1989   973.5'092'4—dc19 [B] [92]   89-3098
                                                                                                   CIP AC

ISBN 0-88062-156-7   Paperbound

CONTENTS

Daniel's Favorite Stories

"It was in April of 1777, just ten short years ago, when two thousand redcoats and German Hessians landed on Long Island Sound and rode through the countryside setting farmhouses on fire. General Arnold heard about it in New Haven and moved into immediate action."

Five-year-old Daniel wriggled closer to his father's feet so as not to miss a single word of the story. Even though he had heard the tales of the War for Independence many times and could practically repeat them word for word, he never tired of listening as Captain Ebenezer Webster recalled his exploits in the revolution.

"General Arnold jumped on his horse and set off for Fairfield to fight the British without a single soldier to help him. But by the time he had ridden those twenty-five miles, more than five hundred men were following him. They knew Benedict Arnold. He wouldn't send them to battle from a safe retreat somewhere from behind the lines. He would lead them, riding right out in front, hurling himself as a flying target against the enemy.''

"Were you riding with him father?" Daniel frowned at his sister Abigail. She never remembered the stories.

"Not that time," Captain Webster smiled. "I met General Arnold later, under much different circumstances. Do you want to hear that story instead?"

"No, Father, please," Daniel pleaded. "Finish this one first. Tell us how his horse was shot from under him and how the British soldier tried to capture him."

Ebenezer laughed. "Maybe you should tell us, Daniel, my boy. You seem to recall every one of my stories, right down to the last detail."

It was true. Daniel was a small boy, and had been sickly ever since he was born. The neighbor ladies who helped his mother when he was born told each other and anyone else who would listen that they didn't think he would make it through his first year. But what he lacked in strength he made up for with his mind. Already at five he could read. His sisters taught him the letters and their sounds and giggled as he sounded out words from the big family Bible and their school books. He never forgot what he read from the books, just as he never forgot one of his father's stories.

Ebenezer rubbed the small lad's head and took up the story again. "Arnold and his volunteers caught up with the redcoats near Ridgefield. The British were off guard, because their scouts had not reported any enemy troops in the area. General Arnold engaged them in battle immediately. He led his men right toward the middle of the line of redcoats who were frantically trying to organize into battle formation. Their horses split the British line in two, scattering

muskets and soldiers in every direction. Those redcoats who had time to load and fire concentrated on
the man leading the unexpected attack and General
Arnold's horse stumbled and fell with nine bullet holes
in him.''

"Oh, the poor thing," Mehitabel murmured. But
Daniel wasn't concerned about horses.

"General Arnold. Tell us about General Arnold."

"Well, when the general's horse fell he tried to jump
free. But his foot got caught in the stirrup. Down he
fell, with the horse on top of him, pinned fast to the
ground. Up rushed a redcoat with a long bayonet on
the end of his rifle pointed right at the general's chest.

" 'You're my prisoner,' he shouted.''

"Not yet," squealed Daniel.

"Not yet." His father grinned at the boy's enthusiasm. "Arnold pulled a pistol from his waistcoat,
shot the British soldier through the chest, and rolled
into the brush under a hail of musket fire, his hat full
of bullet holes. Checking quickly to make certain he
was still in one piece, he crawled out of the bushes,
grabbed the reins of a loose horse, and rallied his
troops for another attack. They chased the British all
the way to Compo Point and back onto their ships.''

Daniel clapped for joy. "Tell us another one ,
Father. Tell us the story of you and Arnold at West
Point."

Captain Ebenezer Webster was the hero of all his
children, but particularly of young Daniel. Ebenezer
was among the first to respond to the call to arms
following the battles of Concord and Lexington. He
mustered a company of two hundred men from their
home town of Salisbury, New Hampshire, which
fought under his command throughout most of the
war.

Ebenezer looked the part of a soldier. He was nearly
six feet tall, yet towered over other men of the same

height because of his confident bearing. His face was so dark that it was said not even burnt gunpowder would change his complexion. His head was big, his features large and prominent. An easy smile and a quick laugh habitually revealed shining teeth, though he also had a frown which the children knew and responded to quickly.

Others, as well, shared the children's respect for their father. Ebenezer had just been elected moderator of the Salisbury town meeting for the nineteenth year in a row. His neighbors would continue to honor him with that office for another twenty-four years. And they had sent him as a delegate to the convention which framed the first New Hampshire constitution and he soon would be going to the convention in which New Hampshire would consider the Constitution of the United States of America.

Even the great General George Washington respected and trusted Ebenezer.

"Please, Father, The West Point story, please."

Ebenezer Webster smiled indulgently at the boy. It was past his bedtime, but it was hard to say no. He knew they spoiled Daniel, but the boy really wasn't strong enough to do hard work around the farm. His brother Ezekiel didn't seem to mind doing his own work and Daniel's too. The girls treated him special, too, doing chores for him in exchange for hearing him quote one of the many Bible verses he had committed to memory. None of them ever tired of listening to enormous words like "resurrection" and "transfiguration" coming from his five-year-old lips.

"Well," Captain Webster began, "my men joined General Washington in Morristown early in 1780. The British were headquartered in New York City and General Arnold had just been given command of our garrison at West Point. He still had not fully recovered from his leg wound and therefore wasn't fit for active duty.

"As commander of West Point, Arnold was in control of half a dozen forts on both sides of the Hudson, twelve miles of the river, and the crossing at King's Ferry, the last remaining passage open to us. It was a strategic post for a man who had turned traitor and was secretly supplying vital information to the British.

"One moonless night Major Andre let down a rowboat from the side of the *Vulture*, a British ship in the Hudson River. He crossed the Hudson and met with General Arnold to make secret plans for the surrender of West Point. While they were meeting, one of Arnold's captains, a friend of mine by the name of Livingston, hauled a howitzer out to the bank of the river and fired on the *Vulture*. The ship sailed away, and the major had to find another way to return to British lines. He changed from his uniform into civilian clothes, put secret documents outlining the defenses of West Point in his boots, and set out."

Daniel hunched his shoulders together and stared up at his father. How he loved to hear his father tell stories. The only thing he liked better was to retell them to his friends later on. When he came to this part of the tale he would always stop and wait for a long time, until his friends begged him to continue. His father kept right on going.

"Along the way, Andre was stopped by a gang of 'skinners,' ruffians who stole from honest citizens under the guise of being part of the army. Andre thought the men were friends, so he told them he was a British officer. When he discovered they were patriots, he pretended he was just testing them and showed his safe conduct pass signed by General Arnold. But the skinners searched him anyway and found the secret papers in his boots. Then they

delivered Andre to the captain of some nearby
American troops.

"All this while, Arnold sat in his house at West
Point waiting for the British to attack so he could surrender to them. Three American officers came with
the news that General Washington and our party were
soon to arrive. Arnold and his wife Peggy served the
officers breakfast. Arnold was excited. Now he could
deliver to the British not only West Point, but the commander of the American forces as well."

"Was Peggy Arnold as pretty as they say, Father?"
asked Abigail. Daniel pursed his lips and scrunched
up his face in an imitation of his father's frown at the
interruption. Girls! All they thought about was pretty
faces and pretty dresses.

"Pretty enough," Ebenezer said. "In the middle
of breakfast, a messenger arrived with a letter. General
Arnold silently read that Andre was captured by the
Americans. He hid his fear and excused himself from
breakfast, saying he must visit the fortifications. Then
he rode madly down to the river. With a pistol to their
heads, he forced several of his soldiers to row him
downriver to the *Vulture*."

Daniel's father continued, "Just about then, I arrived with General Washington and we found the
place in confusion. Mrs. Arnold was in bed in a fit
of delirium. Another messenger was there with a letter for Washington. In it, Major Andre asked for mercy. 'General Arnold has betrayed his country.'
Washington told us. Then he added those words I will
never forget: 'Whom can we trust now?' "

With a big lump in his throat, young Daniel
whispered the words as his father said them, "Whom
can we trust now?" But the most exciting part of the
story was yet to come.

"It was too late in the day for us to travel on, and

the fortifications at West Point were too important to leave, until we were certain they were secure. No one knew for sure how many people were involved in the treachery. All we knew was that General Arnold was a traitor and we had to assume the worst. We assumed that the British knew how weak our position was and could attack that very night. We assumed that they knew Washington himself was there at Arnold's home.''

Daniel sat up straight now, his eyes ablaze. To think that his father had been there on the most dangerous night of the entire war.

"We sent Colonel Hamilton downriver to see if perchance he could overtake the fleeing Arnold. Washington relieved Arnold's assistant of command and replaced him by Colonel Wade. He assigned General Knox to redistribute the artillery for a better defense of West Point. He asked me to stand guard at the door of his room that night. His last words before he retired were for me alone. 'Captain Webster, I believe I can trust you.' ''

Daniel heaved a great sigh. If only he could do some great deed of bravery for his country, maybe General George Washington would say to him, "Daniel Webster, I believe I can trust you."

That night Daniel curled up deep in his featherbed in the cold attic room he shared with his brother Ezekiel. A verse he had learned from the Bible floated through his half-asleep mind. "O my God, I trust in thee: let me not be ashamed, let not mine enemies triumph over me." God had certainly been on the side of his father and General Washington during the war. Benedict Arnold had done his worst, but the patriots won independence anyway. Daniel was proud to be a patriot. Then God and his father and General Washington got all mixed up in his mind, and he was asleep.

Webster's Boy in the New Nation

"Hey, it's Webster's Boy."

Grimy, stubble-chinned men crowded around the porch of Ebenezer's inn while their horses drank from the water trough. Mr. Webster's hospitality, his many daughters, and the chance to visit with the other teamsters who were always around—all of these were good reasons to visit Elms Farm. Another reason was the pleasure of listening to Webster's boy read the Bible.

Daniel still looked quite delicate at ten years of age but his large, dark eyes flashed with energy as he leaned the big family Bible up against the porch railing and read aloud.

"Thou shalt also be a crown of glory in the hand of the Lord, and a royal diadem in the hand of thy God. Thou shalt no more be termed Forsaken; neither shall thy land any more be termed Desolate: but thou shalt be called Hephzibah, and thy land Beulah: for the Lord delighteth in thee."

"That boy ought to be a preacher, he should," the

men muttered to one another. "Reads as good as George Whitfield any day."

"Did you hear the way he said Hephzibah? Why, I don't know what a hephzibah is, but I sure like the way he says it."

"Come on, Dan. Read some more."

So Dan read from Isaiah and Jeremiah, two of his favorite books, and from the Revelation of St. John the Divine. He loved the verses about trumpets and vials and horses and beasts.

"And another angel came out from the altar, which had power over fire," Daniel read to the men in his loudest voice, "and cried with a loud cry to him that had the sharp sickle, saying, Thrust in thy sharp sickle, and gather the clusters of the vine of the earth; for her grapes are fully ripe. And the angel thrust in his sickle into the earth, and gathered the vine of the earth, and cast it into the great winepress of the wrath of God."

When he finished, all the men clapped. None of the preachers they listened to for six hours every Sabbath day read the Bible like Daniel did. He made it exciting.

The Bible wasn't the only book Daniel read, though it was one of his favorites. He read everything he could get his hands on. His job was to run the small sawmill on the farm, which gave him a great deal of time to read. He would set a log on the mill, start the blade and sit down to read. By the time the blade had made one entire cut the length of the log he was many pages further along in his book.

There was a small circulating library in Salisbury but never enough books to satisfy Dan. He read the books so many times that he knew most of them from memory, a fact which aided him on some occasions and got him into trouble on others. Pope's "Essay on Man'' he could repeat from beginning to end, along with many of the psalms and the hymns of Dr. Isaac Watts.

Schoolmaster James Tappan was a favorite of the community school children when he came to their village for his eight-week stay.

"We're going to have a contest during this term," he announced on the first day of school as the eleven girls and five boys who weren't needed in the fields that day took their places on the long, hard benches with copybooks in hand.

"For the person who memorizes the most verses from the Holy Scriptures during the next eight weeks," he said, dramatically holding a brand-new jackknife over head, "This will be the prize."

All the children worked hard, but Daniel had a head start which not even the most diligent effort could overcome. On the day the contest ended, Mr. Tappan had each student come to the front of the room to recite. Someone quoted twenty-five verses. Then one of the older girls beat that by quoting forty and another girl quoted fifty-two Bible verses without a single mistake. Then it was Daniel's turn.

Walking confidently to the front of the little one-room school, he turned to face Mr. Tappan and his classmates.

"I will begin with Psalm 1." The schoolmaster marked them off on the blackboard under Daniel's name. Twelve verses in Psalm 2. Eight in Psalm 3. Twenty-six in all, already more than everyone else with the exception of the two oldest girls.

Eight verses in Psalm 4, twelve more from Psalm 5, ten from Psalm 6. He was in the lead, the obvious winner. But still Daniel didn't stop.

He quoted the seventeen verses of Psalm 7, the nine verses from Psalm 8, twenty from Psalm 9 and eighteen from Psalm 10. One hundred and twenty verses with never a pause and never a single misspoken word!

"Enough," called the schoolmaster as Dan grabbed a quick breath in preparation for starting the eleventh psalm. "I declare Daniel Webster the winner of the jackknife."

There were other times, however, when his ability to memorize got him into trouble. When the yearly almanac arrived, filled with its predictions on the weather, snatches of popular poetry, proverbs and other items of necessary and unnecessary wisdom, it was eagerly passed from one member of the family to the other. Started by Benjamin Franklin, the almanac had rapidly become one of the most popular sources of information in a nation with very few newspapers. Daniel took his turn at reading the almanac, and as usual committed much of it to memory.

"The almanac says the weather this April will be warmer than usual," he whispered to his brother Ezekiel as they snuggled down into their featherbed one night. "I can't wait to start fishing and swimming again over at the old hole."

Ezekiel, too, was excited about the prospects of summer arriving, and they laid awake for several hours discussing their plans.

"Let's go over to the Blackwater Reservoir and borrow a rowboat from Farmer Stevens. Remember those largemouth bass we caught last summer?"

"Great! And I'll take you to meet Robert Wise. You'll like him. He's full of stories about his days in battle. Did you know that he jumped ship in Boston, hid out from the entire British army for a week and then joined a New Hampshire Regiment for the rest of the war? He can take us right into the middle of where the deer are bedded down for the night and they never even know he's there. I think he can make his way through the forest more quietly than an Indian. Maybe he will take us fishing down the Merrimack in his canoe.''

By the time they finished discussing their summer plans it was nearly two o'clock in the morning and Ezekiel knew they would have to be doing chores at the first light of day.

"Guess we'd better be calling it a night," he whispered to his younger brother. "Remember what Ben Franklin said in his almanac, 'Early to bed and early to rise, makes a man healthy and wealthy and wise'.''

Daniel was quiet for a long time and Ezekiel thought he had gone to sleep, so he closed his eyes and dozed off. But instead Daniel was thinking, and before long he poked his brother in the chest.

"I don't think that's what it said.''

Ezekiel rubbed his eyes and groaned himself awake. "What are you talking about?''

"The almanac. I don't think that is what it said.''

"What is what it said?" Ezekiel was exasperated at being awakened and didn't recall what they had been talking about when he fell asleep.

"The almanac. Ben Franklin's. You said, 'Early to bed and early to rise, makes a man healthy, and wealthy and wise.' I don't think that is what it says.''

"Of course it is." Ezekiel was wide awake now, but not very happy about it. "Do you think you are the only one who can remember anything?''

"I didn't say that. I just think you have one word wrong. I think the almanac said, 'Early to bed and early to rise, leaves a man healthy and wealthy and wise.' That's what I think.''

Ezekiel groaned again. Sunrise was going to come

mighty early the next morning. "Well, why don't you go check, and in the meantime let me get some sleep." With that he turned his face toward the wall, effectively ending the conversation.

Daniel didn't really want to climb out of the warm bed, but Ezekiel had made him mad by not believing him. Quietly, so as not to wake anyone else in the house, especially his father, he slipped out from under the covers and sneaked down the stairs and into the parlor where he remembered seeing the almanac the evening before. It was dark, much too dark to read anything even by the moonlight coming through the window. He would have to light a candle.

Shivering in the chill night air he took a piece of flint from the box over the fireplace, set a candle on the floor and proceeded to light it. Opening the almanac he leafed quickly through its pages, searching for the elusive quatrain. There it was, at the head of the page that introduced the month of April. Ezekiel was right. "Early to bed, and early to rise, makes a man healthy, and wealthy and wise."

Disgusted with himself he dropped the book to the floor and scurried back up the stairs to the warmth of his bed. He didn't even wake Ezekiel to tell him. Maybe he would forget the argument by morning and Daniel would never have to admit that he was wrong.

Perhaps no one would ever have known that Daniel was wrong except for one thing. As he dropped the book and ran up the stairs, he knocked the candle to the floor. Soon the rag rug in front of the fireplace was blazing and flames were licking their way along the floor in search of his mother's drapes and the wooded paneled walls of Elms Farm.

Daniel, back in his featherbed, did not know of the fire. But in running up the stairs he had not been as careful as he had in sneaking down to check the almanac. Ebenezer heard the light footsteps. He rose to investigate and discovered a good portion of the parlor in flames.

"Fire!" he yelled. "Fire! Everybody out of the house immediately."

Daniel, still wide awake and horribly aware of what he had done, was the first one down the stairs to join his father in beating at the flames with water-soaked rugs. Ezekiel was right behind him as their mother and the girls in their long nightgowns raced for the door. As soon as the girls were safe, Mrs. Webster came back in. She soaked rugs for the men as they pounded desperately at the fire. She threw buckets of water at the walls to save her drapes, and with their combined efforts the last flame was soon extinguished. In the middle of the blackened corner of the room lay the new almanac, charred almost beyond recognition.

"Daniel," Captain Webster said, frowning that terrible frown which the children all dreaded, "what do you know about this?"

Daniel told the entire story, and soon everyone knew that for once his memory had failed him. He determined never to let it happen again.

When a schoolmaster by the name of William Hoyt announced that he was starting a store in Salisbury it was big news. Before that, store-bought goods had to be purchased in Concord nearly fifteen miles away. Daniel and his sisters walked to town almost every day that first week the store was open just to smell pickles and peppers in open barrels and stare at hard horehound candy in a glass jar on the shelf behind the counter.

It wasn't horehounds that Daniel bought with his first pennies, however. From the first day he had his eye on a small cotton pocket handkerchief decorated with colored flags and military emblems and printed on both sides with the new Constitution of the United States of America.

Ebenezer Webster had gone to the New Hampshire convention, and they ratified the Constitution. As the ninth state to ratify, New Hampshire's vote put the new Constitution into effect, creating the United States of America.

Daniel had heard his father tell of the debate and how he and others like him won the day over those who feared a centralized government and wanted to keep the Articles of Confederation. But he had not seen a copy of the Constitution until Mr. Hoyt opened his store and the handkerchief caught his eye.

Once the handkerchief was in his possession he refused to let go of it even for a washing. He showed it to everyone but lent it to no one. He read it over and over again, enjoying the words and learning the concepts which were to influence him all the rest of his life.

"We the people of the United States, in order to form a more perfect union, establish justice, ensure the domestic tranquility, provide for the common defense, promote the general welfare, and secure the blessings of liberty to ourselves and our posterity, do ordain and establish this Constitution for the United States of America."

We the People...

3

From Farm to Schoolroom

Revival! There was no other way to describe the events of the spring of 1792 at the Congregational church in Salisbury. When a small group of parishioners began to meet every morning for prayer, no one else in the community paid any attention. Four hours of prayer and preaching on Sunday were enough for anyone. When the same group prevailed on the minister, Rev. Thomas Worcester, to bring in a preacher all the way from Boston for an extended meeting, there was some talking, along with some raised eyebrows. After all, Salisbury was already a religious community.

The first night of the meeting families from as far away as Boscawen came, partly to show how religious they were and partly to see who else was there. By the end of the week the only ones still coming were the small group who had met originally to pray. Along with the minister and the visiting preacher they decided to hold one more service the following Monday night.

The audience was small that evening, but after the service a young lady who didn't have a very good reputation in the village went to the altar and prayed for more than an hour. The minister and preacher decided to extend the meeting one more night.

On Tuesday, the lady was back with several of her friends who also went to the altar following the service. Word began to spread around town that something was happening at the Congregational church; young people were making decisions which were changing their lives.

The meeting was in its third week when Ebenezer loaded the Websters into a haywagon and joined the crowd at the church building. It was not that Captain Webster didn't like to go to church. On the contrary, the Websters were there every Sabbath day without fail even though Ebenezer was a Presbyterian and the only church in their village was Congregational. It was just that he was leary of the "emotionalism" he had heard about in connection with revivals. But on the previous Sunday their Rev. Worcester assured him personally that no one yet had waved any handkerchiefs nor had any of the women been allowed to pray out loud.

"I believe you will like our friend from Boston," the minister assured Mr. Webster. "He is a strict Calvinist like ourselves and will never allow any excesses in his meeting, I am sure. But when the Holy Spirit is at work, His people ought to be in attendance."

Monday night of that third week the small frame building in the center of Salisbury was overflowing with people. When the ushers saw Captain Webster unloading his family from the wagon they made certain his pew was ready for him. The previous year his neighbors had voted him as judge for the court of common pleas in the country and ''it wouldn't be fitting for the Judge to have to stand through the service, now would it?'' they whispered to the people who were asked to move.

That evening almost a dozen people gathered at the altar for prayer following the preaching, some of them very prominent people in town. As his father greeted friends and acquaintances outside the church, Daniel stood quietly at the rear of the building gazing at those who were kneeling in prayer. The sermon had affected him greatly and he desired to join those who were making their peace with God.

It was there that his father found him when the family was ready to leave.

''Come along, Daniel. We're waiting for you in the wagon.''

The boy followed his father obediently, but when he climbed into the haywagon he worked his way through the other children to a place immediately behind the hard bench where his parents were sitting.

''Father, should I have joined them at the altar tonight?''

Judge Webster drove quietly for a long time before answering.

''Well, son. Let me ask you this. What have you thought of the preaching you have heard every Sabbath day since you can first recall attending church?''

''Why, father, I believed every word of it. The Sabbath day sermons come from God himself, for they are taken from the text of his Holy Word.''

The judge smiled to himself and continued his questioning. ''And prayer, my son. What have you thought of the prayers?''

''Prayer is conversation with the Father of us all

and a time for great reverence." Daniel didn't have to stop and think about that answer for prayer was as much a part of life in the Webster family as eating and drinking. "I pray myself, every night and often during the day as well, though perhaps not as lengthy as the minister."

Daniel's father grinned openly at the boy's confession. Their minister was known for his long prayers many of which lasted for over an hour, almost at long as his sermons. Then he continued the questions.

"The Holy Scriptures, Daniel. What do you think of the Holy Scriptures?"

"That they are the Word of God," came the prompt reply. "God has given them to us for our doctrine, reproof, correction and instruction in righteousness as says the Apostle Paul in the second epistle written to Timothy."

"Very good, son," Judge Webster beamed his approval. "If I were to render a decision on the merits of your testimony, I would have to conclude that you show every evidence of being a Christian; a belief in the Holy Scriptures, a dependence on prayer and an attendance on the preaching of the Word. Let those of us who know the Lord demonstrate our obedience to Him in the matters of daily living and let those who do not know Him spend time at the altar."

Though the revival continued for several more weeks and the Websters attended almost every night, Daniel never again felt the desire to join the seekers at the altar. He knew he believed in his Father's God and what was good enough for Judge Webster was good enough for his youngest son.

In the years after his father became judge, life at Elms Farm was much easier. The judgeship carried with it a salary of four hundred dollars a year, and

added to the income from the inn and the farm it provided a sustantial increase in the living standard of
the Websters. Although Daniel was not aware of the
decision, Judge Webster began to inquire into the
possibility of providing the boy with more education
than he was able to get from the itinerant teachers
who visited the village a few weeks each year.

Daniel was making his own contribution to the
family income through a part-time job cleaning the
office of a lawyer in Salisbury. Once again his love
for books tempted him to spend more time reading
than working. A small book of Latin grammar on the
lawyer's shelves caught his attention. Every day he
took it down and pored over it's pages, trying to
understand the strange language it was teaching him
to read.

One day the lawyer came into the office while he
was reading.

"Latin, Daniel? I didn't realize you were a
scholar."

Dan wasn't sure if he was angry or was teasing him.
"I'm not sir, and I have all my work done, I hope
you don't mind my reading, sir."

"Not at all. But a Latin grammar? Tell me, what
have you learned from the book?"

To the lawyer's amazement Daniel began to quote
the first chapter from memory, and then the next.
Taking the small volume from the lad his employer
opened it and followed along as the lad quoted page
after page from the grammar. His pronunciation of
the Latin words was atrocious, but his awe at the boy's
retention kept him from laughing.

When Daniel finished, the lawyer handed him the
book.

"It's yours to keep, my boy. I think you'll be using
it some day."

That very evening he made a trip out to Elms Farm to encourage the judge to send his youngest boy to Phillips Exeter Academy where the lawyer had attended school. The judge took it as an answer to his prayers as to where to send Daniel for more training.

Soon after that, on a hot July afternoon, Daniel and his father were working in the hayfields, and the Honorable Abiel Foster of Canterbury came to visit. Mr. Foster, a former minister, was now a member of the Congress of the United States in Philadelphia. Daniel's father had helped him be elected to that office. After Mr. Foster left, Ebenezer called Daniel from his work to join him sitting on a haycock under an elm tree at the edge of the field.

"My son," he said, "Abiel Foster is a worthy man. He is a member of Congress; he goes to Philadelphia and gets six dollars a day while I toil here in this field barely able to scrape by."

Daniel was surprised to hear his father talk that way. He had never thought of his family as poor. But he listened quietly as Mr. Webster continued.

"It is because he had an education. He is college-learned, an advantage which I never had. If I had received his early education, I should have been in Philadelphia in his place. I came near it, as it was. But I missed it, and now I must work here."

For the first time in his life Daniel saw tears in his fathers's eyes and it broke his heart. Throwing his arms around the strong shoulders of his father he, too, began to cry. "My dear father, you shall not work. Ezekiel and I will work for you and will wear our hands out, and you shall rest."

But that was not what Judge Webster had in mind. Gently removing the boy's arms from around his neck he clasped them tightly and looked firmly into Daniel's eyes.

"The work is of no importance to me. I now live but for my children. I could not give your elder brothers the advantages of knowledge, but I can do something for you. Exert yourself, improve your opportunities, learn, learn, and when I am gone, you will not need to go through the hardships which I have undergone, and which have made me an old man before my time."

The next spring, the hard New England winter behind, Judge Webster loaded Daniel into the farm wagon and drove him the nearly fifty miles to Exeter where the Academy was located. Together they entered the office of the principal, Dr. Benjamin Abbott, and Judge Webster said he wanted to enroll Daniel for the coming term.

"What have you read to prepare for enrollment in Phillips Exeter Academy, young man?"

The sudden questions from the stern man behind the huge oak desk caught Daniel by surprise and his reply came out as a stammer.

"Er, nothing sir. That is, I didn't realize I had to prepare. But I have been reading, sir."

"Very well, what is it you have been reading."

"Why a Latin grammar, sir, given me by a lawyer in Salisbury. The hymns of Dr. Watt, Addison's *Spectator,* Alexander Pope's *Essay on Man* and the Bible."

"Paltry preparation for a boy who wants to attend the academy," the headmaster snapped. "No writing or arithmetic? No Greek authors? Very well, read for me in English if you must. The book of Luke, the twenty-second chapter."

Daniel stood to his feet and accepted the large Bible being thrust at him from across the desk. It was much too heavy for him to hold in one hand while he found the chapter so he rested the top against the front of the oak desk. Taking a deep breath he began.

"The Holy Scriptures, the Gospel according to St. Luke, chapter 22."

"*Now the feast of unleavened bread drew nigh, which is called the Passover. And the chief priests and scribes sought how they might kill him; for they feared the people. Then entered Satan into Judas surnamed Iscariot, being of the number of the twelve.*"

As the familiar words traveled through his mind and out through his lips Daniel forgot about the intimidating figure behind the desk. He thought of the teamsters back home at Elms Farm and how they listened when he read to them.

"*Then came the day of unleavened bread, when the passover must be killed. And he sent Peter and John, saying, Go and prepare us the passover, that we may eat.*"

When it came time to turn the page Daniel was so engrossed in the story that he forgot to turn it. To the principal's amazement he continued right on, quoting the rest of the chapter from memory.

When he was finished, Dr. Abbott sat in silence for a time. He spoke far more gently now. "This 'Essay on Man' and the Latin grammar you mentioned reading. Do you know them as well as you know your Bible?"

Daniel nodded.

"Very well. I believe you will do as a pupil here at Exeter. Judge Webster, your son is accepted as a member of the student body. Deposit his belongings in the barracks and have him report to Mr. Thacher for assignment to tutors."

The next five months were the hardest Daniel had ever spent. For one thing, the boys from Concord and

Manchester and Haverhill and Portsmouth wore store-
bought clothes and they laughed at his rustic clothing
and backwoods manners. When he started classes it
was even worse. None of the schoolmasters in
Salisbury had prepared him for the English grammar,
writing and arithmetic he was expected to do at
Exeter. His only Latin was the little grammar he had
memorized, and all the other boys knew at least some
Greek.

The worst embarrassment of all, however, was his
inability to give a declamation.

"Now we will hear from Daniel Webster," Mr.
Buckminster announced after the term had been in
session for two weeks. But Daniel didn't move from
his seat. Joseph Stevens Buckminster was one of his
favorite tutors. He was an older student at the
academy, chosen to give instruction in Latin grammar when Dr. Abbott became ill. He had heard about
the new student's entrance examination and had no
reason to believe the boy would be hesitant to give
an oration, particularly one he had been learning for
two weeks.

"Mr. Webster, will you stand and recite, please?"

But Daniel simply shook his head miserably. He
couldn't, he absolutely couldn't get up in front of all
those swells.

Mr. Buckminster talked with him after class, trying to encourage him. Throughout the term Daniel
met with Mr. Emery and Mr. Thacher and every
other tutor who had him in class. Some of them
frowned and some smiled, but none got any further
than Mr. Buckminster. The boy who had always enjoyed an audience could not bring himself to get up
in front of the students at Exeter and speak. He
quickly mastered the rudiments of English grammar.

In arithmetic and writing he made substantial progress. But a declamation he could not, and would not give.

"Perhaps after the autumn break we will have the privilege of hearing you speak," Joseph Buckminster encouraged him late in October. "I have heard you quote many a piece word for word in your own room so I know you have the ability to memorize. You must overcome this unreasonable fear, Daniel. Declamation is the finest of the arts, the flower of modern civilization. There is no quicker way to achieve recognition among your peers than through the platform."

But the autumn break came and went, the next term began with a heavier load of advanced subjects and still Daniel could not bring himself to speak in public. He committed to memory all the exercises assigned to him. He recited and rehearsed in the privacy of his room. But when the school assembled to hear declamations and his name was called, all eyes would turn to his seat and he found he could not raise himself from it.

An entire year passed at the Phillips Exeter Academy without Daniel ever building up the courage necessary to face his fellow classmates from the platform. It was as if his entire talent in that area had suddenly disappeared.

After a year at Exeter Judge Webster sadly informed Daniel that there wasn't enough money available to send him back for another term, so at fifteen years of age he began teaching in a small one-room school near home. He had received his year of higher education. Any more was unthinkable for the son of a New England farmer, even if he was the county judge. Daniel looked to a future of itinerant teaching, following the footsteps of the men who had taught him in the schools of Salisbury over the years. Inwardly he was glad that at least he would not have to spend his life in the hayfields like his brothers.

We the People...

4

Struggles for an Education

The winter sun sparkled on fresh snow as the Webster sleigh made its way from Elms Farm to Boscawen in February of 1797. Daniel, having taught school in Salisbury during the fall, was once again being given the opportunity to study. This time his tutor was to be Dr. Samuel Wood, a minister in the neighboring village.

Judge Webster guided the team expertly through the snowdrifts. "Dr. Wood seemed quite impressed with the reports he received of your teaching," he said.

Daniel said nothing. He hadn't particularly enjoyed teaching school, but he had tried to do better than some of the teachers who taught him.

"You know that Dr. Wood had tutored well over one hundred boys during his ministry. Most of them have gone on to college."

A chill went up Daniel's spine, which had nothing to do with the cold weather and he turned to search his father's face. But the judge was watching the road before them, not looking at his son. Never in Daniel's wildest dreams had he considered going to college. Only preachers and doctors and lawyers went to college. He thought he was going to study with Dr. Wood only so he could return to the schoolroom and teach the next term.

"College, father?" he whispered.

"Dartmouth, where Dr. Wood was graduated from. He tells me that it is his opinion you can be prepared to do well at college but it will mean much study on your part. He is charging me a dollar a week for your lodging, board and instruction. It is a steep fee, but I can hardly expect him to do it for nothing. I live only for you children, son, and if you will promise to do all you can for yourself, I will do what I can for you."

His father was still not looking at him but was keeping his eyes on the horses and the road ahead. Daniel's head grew dizzy as he thought of the sacrifice that was being made for him. First the cost of Dr. Wood's tutoring, then the cost of the years at Dartmouth. Reaching out he placed his hands over the rough, calloused hands of his father which held the reins, and laying his head on his father's strong shoulder, he wept. His tears were of love, of gratitude and of joy.

Even after Daniel's year at Exeter there were many subjects which he would be expected to be familiar with in college which as yet he had not studied. He would be studying six months with Dr. Wood.

"We will begin," Dr. Wood announced the first day, "with Latin. You will translate ten pages every day from Virgil and ten from Cicero. Before breakfast. Then we will discuss them as we break our fast together."

The first few mornings, breakfast was very late as Daniel struggled with the Latin nouns and verbs. But as he grew more familiar with what the authors were saying the translation went faster. Cicero in particular became a pleasure so that he looked forward to his translation work as much as he did to eating, and it no longer seemed like a hard task at all.

Cicero was one of Daniel's favorites because of the way he used speaking ability to help the people of Sicily. Gaius Verres, a robber governing the island of Sicily, was brought to trial and Cicero took the case on behalf of the people of the island. When Cicero finished speaking against Verres the governor didn't even wait for the verdict. He simply left the island and went into exile, knowing there was no way he could answer the arguments of Cicero. Daniel could think of no better use of a speaking ability to speak than on behalf of a people against a corrupt government. To him the speeches of Cicero were just like the speeches of Patrick Henry and Samuel Adams against the British crown.

One of the first works by Cicero which Daniel translated was the "First Oration Against Catiline." In that speech Cicero crushed a conspiracy which Catiline was making against the Roman republic. As Daniel discussed the speech with Dr. Wood at breakfast they began to talk as well of General George Washington, who was the new President of the United States. Dr. Wood, like Judge Webster, was a Federalist who felt that Washington was the only man qualified to lead the new republic in the right direction. Daniel's respect for the President grew rapidly as he compared him to Cicero and studied the problems which faced the Roman republic in the first century.

After breakfast and the discussion of Latin classics, came mathematics. Daniel had done well at Exeter in arithmetic and was surprised to discover how much there was yet to learn. Higher mathematics came

easily because it was logical, though he never thought
it a pleasure like literature. Geography and history
were discussed just before noon meal if there was time.

The afternoons Dr. Wood reserved for his sermon
preparation while Daniel was expected to continue
studying on his own at the Boscawen Social Library.
The Boscawen Library was much larger than the one
in Salisbury and had almost two hundred books. To
his delight Daniel discovered many other writings by
his old favorite Alexander Pope, whose "Essay on
Man" he had once memorized. He read the poetry
of John Milton and the Olney hymns of William
Cowper. Some of these he memorized to quote for
the Wood's family as they gathered for their evening
time of hymn singing and Bible reading. William
Cowper was one of the family's favorites.

> "*Sometimes a light surprises*
>   *The Christian while he sings;*
> *It is the Lord who rises*
>   *With the healing on His wings;*
> *When comforts are declining,*
>   *He grants the soul again*
> *A season of clear shining*
>   *To cheer it after rain.*
>
> *In holy contemplation*
>   *We sweetly then pursue*
> *The theme of God's salvation*
>   *And find it ever new;*
> *Set free from present sorrow,*
>   *We cheerfully can say,*
> *E'en let the unknown tomorrow*
>   *Bring with it what it may!*
>
> *It can bring with it nothing,*
>   *But He will bear us through;*
> *Who gives the lilies clothing*

Will clothe his people too;
Beneath the spreading heavens
No creature but is fed;
And He who feeds the ravens
Will give His children bread.

Though vine nor fig tree neither
Their wonted fruit shall bear
Though all the field should wither,
Nor flocks nor herds be there:
Yet God the same abiding,
His praise shall tune my voice;
For, while in Him confiding,
I cannot but rejoice."

Daniel read through the library one book after another, setting aside only those written in Greek, which he had not yet studied. If books were in Latin, he translated them. If they were too long to read in a single afternoon he put a marker in his place and continued the next day. Whatever he read he discussed with Dr. Wood during the evening meal, and whatever he memorized he quoted for the family following dinner.

One day he started to read Cervantes' *Don Quixote*. Soon he was totally lost in a world of windmills and castles, knights in armor and fair maidens in distress. When Dr. Wood and his family gathered for the evening meal, Daniel was not there. After they finished eating, one of the children found him under a tree in front of the library, still reading his book. The library had been closed for hours and Daniel had no idea how he moved from inside to out under the tree. He wasn't hungry and hadn't even realized it was time to eat. A good book was more important than food.

During the summer Daniel made the trip home to

Salisbury to help with the haying. It was fun to see the family again, but more than before the work in the fields chafed him. He much preferred to sit alongside the brook and read Milton or translate Cicero than to throw bales of hay. After two weeks his father sent him back to Boscawen, even stronger in his conviction Daniel must be prepared for some other work than farming.

"One area of study still remains, before you will be prepared for college," Dr. Wood announced soon after he returned. "I have arranged for a young man, a senior at Dartmouth, to tutor you in Greek. I expect you to apply yourself to your studies with Mr. Palmer with the same diligence that you have given to your studies with me."

The stern admonition was not necesssary, for Daniel was anxious to begin. The only books which he had not read in the entire Boscawen Social Library were those in Greek.

By early August he had read the four Gospels in their original Greek language, and Dr. Wood announced that he was satisfied with the progress his pupil had made. He recommended to Judge Webster that the boy be enrolled in Dartmouth College. Daniel was still only fifteen years old.

Just before the fall term began that August, Daniel Webster rode into Hanover, New Hampshire, on his horse, a featherbed tied behind him on the saddle. He was four years younger than most of the freshmen. His head was crammed with the knowledge Dr. Wood had given him during the previous six months and he was ready to make his mark in the world.

Hanover was in the mountains, cut out of a pine forest. Though the college had nearly one hundred fifty students and was one of the largest in the new nation, the students did not look down on Daniel because of his clothes. They were willing to give him an equal chance, and he quickly gained their friendship and acceptance.

There were two literary societies on campus in 1797 and the young freshman was accepted into one of them, the United Fraternity, almost immediately. They began to meet in his room and even elected him to an office, something unheard of for a freshman. The main area of competition between the students was in oratory rather than sports. It soon became evident to his friends that public speaking was where Daniel was going to excel.

"Mr. Webster will now read to the class a poem he has written concerning the wars between the British and the French."

With the eyes of the rest of the freshman class on him, a brief taste of the fear which had overcome him at Exeter returned, but pushing it aside he rose to his feet and began to read. Hesitantly at first, then growing more confident as he read, he told the story of an imaginary battle between a British and a French frigate. The class sat hypnotized, not so much by the words, for it was not great poetry, but by the way in which the words were spoken. His voice grew richer and fuller as he spoke and the excitement of the battle gripped the audience. His oral description brought the scene to life. When he finished, the entire class applauded, but especially the boys from the United Fraternity. Here was a fellow society member who would soon lead them to victory in oratory.

Studies during the freshman year at Dartmouth consisted mainly of translating from Latin and Greek as he had been doing at Dr. Wood's. Latin was coming easily by now and even with the time spent in reading through the Greek New Testament there was much time available for other activities.

In fact, Daniel had more free time than most of the students because of his unusual ability to memorize. He could focus all of his mind on a single subject when he wanted to do so. Where other students needed to fill their notebooks with information and study it for hours, Daniel needed only to be sure that he understood it clearly the first time. He could begin his preparation for a test or a class discussion at the last hour and still do well.

"How can you do it?" they asked him. "You read twenty pages and can nearly quote it word for word."

Daniel shrugged. "I like to read. And what I read, I make my own. When a half hour, or at the most an hour, has passed, I close the book and think over what I have read. If there was anything peculiarly interesting or striking in the passage I try to recall it and lay it up in my memory. Then if that subject comes up in conversation or debate I can talk easily about what I have read."

Reading was the way the new freshman occupied most of his spare time. Often it kept him out of the troubles other students got into. Villagers in Hanover allowed their cattle to graze freely all over town, including the great grassy common on the Dartmouth campus. Some students grew tired of picking cow dung off their shoes, however. One night they herded up every loose cow they could find and drove them down to the Connecticut River and over into Vermont.

President Wheelock, whose long, hooked nose was a favorite subject for jokes among the students, did not look on the disappearance of the cows with favor. Daniel was thankful he had been too busy to join in the fun.

Not that he was always reading. Once a student played a practical joke on him, dousing him with a bucket of water, and in return Daniel knocked the boy's room door off its hinges.

Subjects not being studied in classes were the ones which seemed to interest Daniel the most. In the college library he read extensively in English literature and history. These subjects the students debated in their rooms, while in the classrooms they recited Latin and Greek and discussed Jonathan Edward's essay on free will and John Locke's essay on *"Human Understanding."*

During Daniel's sophomore year the course of study included higher mathematics, which Daniel despised, and classical Greek, which he tolerated. In their rooms the boys debated on the presidency of John Adams and the battles of Napoleon Bonaparte, the Duke of York and Emperor Paul of Russia.

Back home in Salisbury, during spring vacation in 1799, the discussion was on an entirely different topic.

"I've been thinking of leaving home," his older brother Ezekiel confided one night after the rest of the family had gone to bed.

"Where would you go?" Daniel asked. Leaving home was unthinkable to him, even though he realized that at Ezekiel's age his father had been on his own for five years and had already fought in several battles.

"To Ohio, most likely. You can homestead out there for practically nothing."

"But what will Father say? You know he needs you here on the farm. What would Mother and the girls do if something were to happen to him?"

"I know." Ezekiel looked as discouraged as Daniel could ever remember seeing him. "That's why I haven't left. I know I'm needed here. I don't mind working and seeing you go to college; don't get me wrong. But seeing all that you are learning just makes me want more than a life of baling hay and following horses around the field."

Daniel nodded gravely. "I know Ezekiel, though I didn't realize you felt that way too. "Why don't you go back to school? Didn't I hear mother say that a new academy has been started here in Salisbury?"

"How could I do that?" It's all Father can do to pay for your schooling at Dartmouth. If I go to Ohio I could make a fortune and send back enough for mother and the girls to live on as well."

The younger brother shook his head, his mind made up, "No. You need to go to school. First the academy, then Dr. Wood and then Dartmouth, just like me. I've felt badly ever since I went to Exeter that you had to stay here and work so I could go to school. I would have done something about it sooner had I realized it meant so much to you."

"Do you really think I could?" Ezekiel was hesitant, but hopeful, bolstered by the enthusiasm of his brother.

"Of course you can. I'll teach you myself, during vacations. I'll even teach school if necessary, and take more than my four years to finish college. But it's settled. You are going to college if I have to pay for it myself."

The rest of the night the boys sat up talking, making plans and deciding how best to introduce the subject to their father. He was growing older, his health was poor and two of their sisters were still unmarried.

The next day they approached him nervously and Daniel broached the plan explaining how he was willing to keep school and postpone his own graduation should it become necessary. Their father was in favor of the idea immediately.

"Daniel, as I told you before, I live but for you children. What I have is of no value to me except as it can be useful to you. To carry both of you through college may cost everything we have and if so that is of no concern to me. However, it is a serious matter to your mother and sisters, and I feel we should discuss it also with them.''

In the family conference which followed, Mrs. Webster echoed her husband's thoughts. She was willing to mortgage the farm or even sell it if necessary so the two boys could go to college. So Daniel went back to Dartmouth, not only to school, but also to look for work, pleased that his brother Ezekiel would one day be joining him on campus.

We the People...

5

Daniel's Tribute to George Washington

When Daniel returned to Hanover for his junior year he began to look for a job. Still not overly fond of working with his hands, he applied and was accepted as ths superintendent of publications for a small weekly newspaper, the *Dartmouth Gazette* His work consisted of choosing articles from books and current magazines for publication in the newspaper, occasionally including an item he had written personally. With the income from this job he was able to pay his own boarding costs which was greatly appreciated at home, since Ebenezer was now paying for Ezekiel's studies at the academy in Salisbury as well. He also made plans to teach school again during the winter vacation, setting that money aside to pay for Ezekiel's tutoring by Dr. Wood. He was determined that his brother should come to Dartmouth as soon as was possible.

Although the major part of classroom study was still

the Latin and Greek classics, Daniel found his interest growing in another direction—history. He read everything he could find about Britain and France and Russia. He followed the wars of Napoleon and the Duke of York with avid interest. But the history which was taking place right around him was the most exciting of all. Alexander Hamilton supported the undeclared war with France in opposition to President Adams who was trying to negotiate a peace treaty. Daniel, like his father, was a strong Federalist who supported the President. But the division between Hamilton and Adams was clearly destroying the Federalist party and making it possible for Thomas Jefferson and his Democratic-Republicans to gain power in Congress.

December 14, 1799, former President George Washington died after falling ill as a result of riding horseback in snow and sleet.

"How I would love to have a chance to pay tribute to Mr. Washington." Daniel confided to his roommate Aaron Loveland when they returned from the winter vacation that year. "If only there were some way of doing it."

"How about the newspaper or the school literary paper?"

"I don't think so. The *Gazette* is interested mainly in reprints and the literary paper in poetry. I have a new poem for George Herbert which will appear in February. No, Mr. Washington deserves a speech, a larger audience, a grand occasion."

"An oration before the United Fraternity perhaps?" Aaron was trying to be helpful though he sometimes found the ambition of his roommate hard to understand. Most of the students at Dartmouth would have been satisfied with being considered by everyone to be the best in debate and oratory. Daniel always had a greater goal in mind and was disappointed when faculty members chose anyone else to speak on special days. Whenever a discussion took place in the rooms Daniel was right in the middle of the argument. In fact, Aaron sometimes felt like Daniel wasn't arguing with the other students at Dartmouth at all. He had the feeling that Daniel was really arguing with Hamilton and Jefferson and the other men in public life about whom he was always reading.

Other students at Dartmouth felt the same way. It was fun to hear Daniel speak. He had grown rapidly that year and was now tall and thin. His dark skin and large deep-set eyes made him look impressive. He would enter a room or the debating hall and stand quietly, listening to others speak for a time. But everyone knew he was there. Then he would say something in a low voice, almost as if he was just waking up from a deep sleep. The room would grow quiet as others strained to listen. When he had everyone's attention his voice would grow stronger and his words would begin to pour out rapidly and with great power. He always had the latest information on any topic and could pull out from his memory long quotations from Adams and Washington as well as from Cicero and Milton and the Bible. It was assumed when Daniel was in a debate that the United Fraternity would win hands down.

In preparation for his speaking Daniel read speeches by Edmund Burke and the Earl of Chatham, great British orators. He studied the debates of the Constitutional Ratification Conventions as well as those taking place in Congress. One of his favorite books on speech was a new one by Richard Whately called *Elements of Rhetoric*. He particularly liked Whately's book because it did not teach the extremely formal style of elocution which was so popular then in both England and America. Some of his classmates were taking elocution lessons. They studied closely which hand movements were used to make each point in a speech and mechanically used those gestures at the right time. Daniel preferred the natural style of delivery which Whately taught in his book.

Along with his new growth had come the need for new clothes. Remembering his days at Exeter, Daniel decided the days of going around in homespun trousers were over.

"Cotton stockings, silk gloves and velvet trousers!" Aaron exclaimed as his roommate came in after a trip to town. "Aren't you a dandy."

"Just the latest from Richard Lang's General Store," Daniel grinned at the teasing. "My old clothes weren't much better than knickerbockers the way I've been growing. Do you think they will know me back in Salisbury?"

"I doubt it. But what I want to know is how you could afford them, or do you have a gold mine you haven't told me about?" Aaron was well aware of the financial straits of the Webster family and knew that every extra dollar Daniel made was sent home to help with Ezekiel's education.

"Mr. Lang was gracious enough to advance me the money. My account is good with him you know."

"Well I don't know about it being good, but it is large. You must owe the General Store as much as any student at Dartmouth."

Daniel shrugged. "I suppose I do. But I needed new clothes and now I have them." Money was never a big concern to Daniel. If people would lend it to him, all the better. Someday he would make a good salary and pay it all back.

He was working at his desk at the *Gazette* during the spring of 1800 when a delegation of men from the

Hanover City Council approached him.

"Mr. Webster?"

Daniel looked up from his work and then stood to his feet wondering what these men wanted with him.

"Mr. Webster, the city of Hanover has a fine tradition of commemorating the signing of the Declaration of Independence. As you are well aware, we have for twenty-four years set aside the fourth day of July as a day of celebration of that momentous event in 1776."

The speaker paused as if expecting a response and then continued when Daniel nodded his head.

"From the beginning of this tradition we have made an effort to choose as orator for the day one of the finest speakers of our fair city to remind us of the glory of our nation and this document which became the basis of our glorious battle for freedom. Often it has been one who fought in the battles of the revolution, who stalked the British at Lexington and Concord or participated in the surrender of Cornwallis at Yorktown. This year, however, it has come to our attention that one of the students at our own Dartmouth College, an institution which makes every citizen of Hanover proud, has shown a talent in oratory which should by rights be shared with the city at large. Mr. Webster, we have come to invite you to present the Fourth of July Oration for the city of Hanover this coming summer."

Not since the days at Exeter had Daniel been at such a loss for words, but he finally managed to accept the invitation. "It will be my privilege to speak," he told the delegation gravely.

The spirit with which he told Aaron about the invitation when he returned to their room was not grave at all.

"It's my chance, my opportunity," he exclaimed.

"I shall speak of President Washington and his unexcelled contribution to the cause of freedom. I shall warn the people against the growth of Jeffersonian republicanism and Hamiltonian warmongering. I shall proclaim the greatness of the Constitution and give due credit to the God of Heaven who superintends the affairs of all nations."

Aaron was impressed. "The Fourth of July Oration? You know that no Dartmouth student has ever before been asked to give it."

Daniel nodded solemnly. It was a great opportunity and he planned to make the best of it.

For the classroom discussions Daniel practiced his off-hand speaking, talking on subjects he had read about and not making any intensive preparation. For the formal debates he prepared by meditating upon the subject and making notes, though he never carried the notes to the lectern with him. For this speech, he studied, meditated, and wrote it out word for word, anticipating the fact that the newspapers would want to publish it. Then he memorized the entire oration and practiced in his room and out in the fields near town until every word was in place. The fear which had controlled him at Exeter was now his servant, driving him to such thorough preparation that there was no possibility of failure.

The day of the celebration all classes were canceled at the college and students joined the citizens of Hanover for games, fireworks and a picnic on the village square with food enough for even the largest of student appetites. The entire afternoon was given over to speech-making. A representative from each class in the common school spoke first. These were followed by the members of the clergy. Late in the afternoon it was time for the final oration.

As Daniel rose from his place among the Dartmouth

students and made his way to the platform which had been erected at one end of the green, the entire student body rose to their feet, clapping and cheering. It was a great honor for all of them to have a member of the student body chosen for this occasion.

Without a note in his hands Webster walked confidently onto the platform and turned to face the crowd. The entire Dartmouth student body, the city councilmen who had invited him to speak, the clergymen and almost everyone in the village sat quietly before him, waiting to hear what he had to say. It was a thrilling feeling.

The people of Hanover expected a Fourth of July speech to begin with a recital of the exciting events of the revolution, events which many of them remembered, and Daniel did not disappoint them. In vivid language, remembering the stories he had heard so often from his father, he described the heroes of the war for independence, reminding his audience of the gallantry of their own husbands and fathers who had fought with General Gates, General Washington, Lafayette and others.

Then, as he told his roommate he would, Daniel launched into a moving tribute to Washington, lamenting his passing and describing him as "the man, who never felt a wound, but when it pierced his country, who never groaned, but when fair freedom bled." Many were in tears as together they mourned the loss of their nation's first president.

From there, the boy orator turned to the national and international scene, praising President Adams, though he knew there were many supporters of Hamilton in the crowd, and warning not only Hanover, but also the nation, of the dangers of the French Directory. Daniel's voice grew strong and his tone majestic as he proclaimed that Napoleon would never "dictate terms to sovereign America." His defiance of the French dictator was cheered long and lustily.

Finally he spoke about the union, this great nation which was so young and so frail yet so loved by them all. He warned of the possibility of a civil war if the various parts of the country were not willing to work together. He advocated support for the new Constitution as the means of keeping the nation united and praised the new order which had come about since the Constitution had been adopted.

It was a good speech for an eighteen-year old boy to give, and if at times he used big words like "supercilious, fire-headed Directory," and "gasconading pilgrim of Egypt" to try to impress his college professors, the people were willing to forgive him. Hanover was happy that they had invited Daniel Webster to speak and Daniel Webster was happy to have been invited.

During his last two years in college Daniel was surrounded by a close group of admirers who recognized something great in him and would agree to nothing new unless it was approved by Webster.

A group of students were playing ball on the college common one afternoon when a businessman from town approached.

"Tell me," said the businessman to one of the students. "Do you think there would be an interest among you students in a dancing school here in town?

I have a mind to begin one if I could anticipate its use by the students of Dartmouth.''

"A dancing school?'' repeated the student.

"Yes, of course. They are the latest thing down in Boston and New York. It would provide an opportunity for you to meet some of the fine young ladies of Hanover, besides being an excellent form of exercise. What do you think?''

Instead of giving him an answer the student returned to the ball game with the reply, ''I'll have to consult with Webster.''

During his senior year the United Fraternity made Daniel its president. His reputation as the greatest orator the school had ever seen was assured by numerous victories in debate as well as other orations.

One of his best speeches was given on a very sad occasion, however. In June of his senior year a classmate by the name of Ephraim Simonds became sick and died. The entire college was saddened and sobered by the unexpected death of such a fine young man and one they had all known. Daniel was asked to deliver a eulogy at the memorial service held at the college.

This time there were no big words and no attempt to impress the professors. He spoke simply but eloquently, with great feeling, about the young man they had known and lost so early in life. In particular, he recalled Ephraim's strong religious faith which had been a testimony to all of them.

As he prepared and delivered the speech he thought of his own religious training; the constant church attendance, the family prayers at home and at Dr. Wood's, and the revival which had swept through Salisbury when he was ten. He realized that he had not thought much about the Lord during his college years, had not read the Bible as he had when it was almost the only book available to read. Now there were many other books to take its place. He could not escape thinking that it could well have been him who was being eulogized, rather than Ephraim Simonds, and that was a sobering thought. In his speech he appealed to his listeners to share the faith of their friend and in his heart he determined to do exactly that.

During the spring term of 1801 a dream was realized as his brother Ezekiel joined him as a Dartmouth student. Two years in the academy at Salisbury and nine months of diligent study under Dr. Wood had prepared him for his entrance examinations in record time. In fact, Ezekiel quickly proved himself to be the student which his brother Daniel was not. Where Daniel prepared for the recitation room, Ezekiel prepared for the classroom. He finished college in only three years, ranked at the top of his class.

Daniel's graduation came in the fall of 1801 and he was not ranked at the top of his class. The two commencement orations were traditionally given by the two top students academically and it was a great disappointment to him that he was not invited to address the students at his own commencement. Instead Thomas Merrill and Caleb Tenney, both of whom ranked above Webster in the class, were asked to give the Latin oration and the valedictory address.

In a letter to a friend from Exeter days Daniel tried to make a joke about the whole day, saying that if people were calling the commencement something for which an apology was necessary, ''it is because they discouraged genius.''

Even without speaking, however, he accepted his diploma and returned home to Salisbury, saddened to leave his college years and unsure of what the future held. Thomas Jefferson was now the President of the

United States, a circumstance which the Federalists believed would ruin the country. James Madison was Secretary of State and Pasha Karamanli of Tripolitania had just declared war on the United States because of the response of the navy to the Barbary pirates.

It was one thing to retell stories of Revolutionary War heroes and another thing entirely to consider the possibility of going to war himself. Daniel was only nineteen, but at that age his father had fought in many battles, and if necessary he would do the same. He was ready to do whatever his country called on him to do.

We the People...

6

A Dream of Boston

Only three choices were open to college educated men when Daniel Webster graduated from Dartmouth. He had never felt a call to the gospel ministry, though Dr. Wood and others had suggested his speaking ability would be a valuable asset in the puplit. Medicine would not afford him the opportunity to speak, which he knew to be his strong suit. That left the legal profession. When the battles with the Barbary pirates did not develop into a full-scale war, Daniel returned to Salisbury and entered the law office of Thomas Thompson. There he would read in preparation for a career as a lawyer.

But Daniel was not anxious to become a lawyer. Before the revolution, most of the leading lawyers has been Royalists, defending the rights of the British crown. After the war there were great problems with debts, and the lawyers were often thought responsible for the fact that many soldiers who had fought patriotically for their nation were now in debt because they had lost their homes and farms in the war and couldn't pay their bills. So lawyers were not held in the same esteem as ministers and doctors. In fact, common terms used to describe the lawyers of that day were "bandits," "vampires," and "windbags."

To his old friend Jeremy Bingham, Daniel wrote that, "to be honest, to be capable, to be faithful to my client and my conscience, I earnestly hope will be my first endeavor." He did not like the idea of making money from the troubles of other people. One of his first jobs for Mr. Thompson was to bring charges against one of the neighboring farmers who had smashed a fiddler's violin at a husking dance.

No one was teaching law at that time. A man prepared for the profession by working as a clerk for an established lawyer in return for the privilege of reading his books. Although Daniel had been able to read most any book in the Dartmouth College library at one sitting and remember it, he found that was not the case with Mr. Thompson's law books. One of the worst was *Coke on Littleton*. He read and reread that book but found it impossible to understand. He much preferred Milton and Cowper and Shakespeare, but he stayed with the law texts, knowing that he would need a thorough understanding of the law in order to succeed in the court system.

Mr. Thompson was a graduate of Harvard and had served as a tutor for three years at that college. In addition to Coke he had Blackstone, Montesquieu and many of the other legal volumes available. Daniel made his way through all of them while at the same time continuing to read the *Iliad*, *Paradise Lost*, Shakespeare's plays, and history books.

The one thing which kept Daniel reading the hard and dry law books was the inner feeling that God had something great for him to do. Sometimes he called it "the fame's curse" and wrote to his friends that he had no desire to be any more than a country lawyer. But at the same time he admitted that there was an urge within him to become famous. It would be safe to settle down in Salisbury and be a country lawyer, but he knew that would not satisfy the ambition within him to use the talents Heaven had given him to their fullest extent.

"Daniel, I'm pleased that you have chosen to study law," Judge Webster told his youngest son after he had been with Mr. Thompson for several months. "But I'm afraid we must find some other source of income if we are to keep your brother Ezekiel in college this term. I have been made aware of a position in Fryeburg, Maine, and was wondering . . . "

Daniel didn't even let him finish the sentence. "Of course, Father. We can't let Ezekiel drop out of school when he has only just begun. Of course I will teach school again. You needn't mention it further."

Fryeburg was a prosperous farming and lumbering center in the Saco Valley, and they offered their new schoolmaster one hundred and seventy-five dollars for the six-month school term. Daniel made arrangements to room with a Dartmouth friend, James McGaw, in the home of Mr. James Osgood, the county registrar of deeds.

"If you would consider my proposal," Mr. Osgood told him the first day, "there is perhaps a way you can pay for your board and room without dipping into your salary."

"That sounds good to me," Webster agreed.

"Well, I would be willing to pay you to make copies of the deeds I write at the price of one shilling and sixpence for each deed."

Daniel made some quick calculations in his head. If he could copy two such deeds each evening he would make a half dollar. Four evenings a week would bring two dollars and that would pay for his board.

"Agreed," he shook hands with Mr. Osgood. "That sound like an offer I cannot refuse."

It did sound like a good deal, until he started writing. He taught school all day, came home for the evening meal, and then sat down at a table to write. The deeds were long and it was important to be extremely careful and to write with a neat hand. He could do two deeds an evening, but the hours were long.

"I hate it," he confided to James McGaw. "The ache never goes out of my fingers. Nothing has ever been such a labor to me as this copying. It is drudgery of the dreariest sort."

"Then why do it?" came the reply. "They pay you enough at the school to cover your board. Why put yourself through the distress?"

"There is only one reason. Ezekiel. I am determined to see him through college with the same opportunities which I enjoyed. As father is now almost without any income at all it is up to me to provide for my brother. Nothing else would compel me to continue this work, I assure you."

The teaching portion of his work Daniel began to enjoy. The students were pleasant to work with and their parents were impressed with their progress, particularly in the area of oratory. The traditional spring program, full of speaking exercises was a great success. Almost from the time he arrived they began asking him to consider staying on in Fryeburg as the permanent schoolmaster.

When a week of vacation came, after the first quarter, Daniel saddled a horse and rode over to Hanover to visit Dartmouth and see his brother. His former classmates were eager to see him and greeted him affectionately. But his real purpose was to help pay Ezekiel's school bill. He could hardly wait until they were alone in his brother's room.

"Look at this Ezekiel," he said, pulling a roll of bills and a stack of coins from his pocket. "Eighty-seven dollars and fifty cents. My salary for an entire quarter of teaching school."

"But what did you live on? What did you eat?" His brother was amazed at the money spread out before him.

Daniel shrugged. "The Lord provided," he said. Then he felt himself enveloped in his brother's strong arms as Ezekiel gave him thanks he couldn't find words to say.

Back in Fryeburg Daniel again determined to save his entire salary for Ezekiel, but this quarter some expenses arose which could not be covered by the two dollars a week he made writing deeds. Refusing to give up his goal, he sold first his horse and then his watch so he would not have to use the money he was putting away for Ezekiel's college fund.

In spite of being constantly without money, Daniel wrote to Jeremy that, "nothing here is unpleasant. The people treat me with kindness and I have the opportunity to find myself in a very good family."

The people of Fryeburg had a good reason to be pleasant to the new schoolteacher, for their children were devoted to him and were accomplishing more than in any previous year of the school. At the time of the second academy exhibitions the speeches of the students were so outstanding that the trustees of the school voted to give a special gift of money to Mr. Webster for his good work. That too he put away for Ezekiel.

His students had a name for Daniel Webster. They called him "All-eyes". For those who tried to get away with mischief behind his back it had a special meaning.

But for most of the students it was a reference to the fact that though he was still quite thin of face, his eyes were large and impressive.

Every morning as class began and every evening before they were dismissed, Daniel led the entire student body in prayer. His voice was deep and his tone somber and many of the students felt as if he were taking themdirectly into the presence of God. Many years later it was his prayers which were remembered the most by those who were in his classroom.

From a Fryeburg attorney, Mr. Judah Dana, he borrowed a set of Blackstone in order to continue his reading in the law. From the circulating library he obtained Adam's *Defense of the American Constitution*, Goldsmith's *History of England* and Mosheim's *Ecclesiastical History*. There, too, he found Fisher Ame's memorable speech on the Jay Treaty which he not only read but memorized. Although college was over, he was just beginning to learn all that he wished to know. He committed to memory long passages from Cicero, and he kept up his languages by translating the odes of Horace into English rhyme.

Though he was enjoying Fryeburg and his teaching, the decision to enter the field of law still weighed heavily upon him. Realizing the disdain with which the profession was held, he wanted to attain a higher goal than many of the men who were then practicing law. His moral upbringing and convictions would not allow him to become a lawyer for the purpose of cheating others out of their possessions. He believed that on any occasion where a man used his ability to speak in order to persuade other men, that man must first of all be honest. A speaker had a primary responsibility to seek the best for all who listened to him.

Summer approached and with it the end of the six months for which Daniel had been hired. He was approached by the trustees of the school, who were also the prominent men in the town.

"We find ourselves extremely well pleased with your conduct of the academy," they told him. "In fact, we are so pleased that we would like to offer you a twelve-month contract at a salary of six hundred dollars, plus a house and a parcel of land."

Daniel almost gasped. The salary figure was almost twice what they were already paying him even without the house.

"Furthermore, knowing of your desire to continue training for the law, we have made arrangements for you to serve as clerk of the court of common pleas for the county of Oxford."

Still Daniel looked at the men and could find nothing to say. It was a wonderful opportunity.

"Thirdly, we would consider it a privilege to have you deliver the Fourth of July oration at our celebration this coming month."

Finally the schoolmaster found his tongue. "I would be pleased to accept, the invitation to speak, that is. As to the other I will consider your offer and let you know. But I will have to have time."

Never before had Daniel been faced with such a difficult decision. If he stayed on as academy master he could support both his father and Ezekiel. It would mean the end of his money problems, but it would very likely mean the end of his career as a lawyer as well. Teaching school would not leave a great deal of time to read law books in preparation for his bar examination.

In spite of the generous offer of the trustees, Daniel's father, Ezekiel and many of his friends encouraged him not to stay. They knew, perhaps better than he did, that he was not called to spend the rest of his life teaching school. It was one thing to do it for a time and something else entirely to contemplate school teaching as a prolonged future.

Daniel stayed to deliver the Fourth of July oration, a speech in which he spoke long and fervently about the glories of the Constitution, and then returned to Salisbury to care for his father and read law once again in the office of Mr. Thompson.

In a letter to Jeremy he said he was returning to the study of law on a trial basis at the insistence of his father. But in turning down the offer of the trustees of Fryeburg Academy he had made a decision which, though it seemed hard at the time, would bring him eventually to a place of great service to his nation.

Without Daniel's teaching salary the financial condition of the Webster family became more desperate. Mr. Thompson was not charging Daniel for the use of his books, but with the exception of Judge Webster's meager salary for his work in the court which came to about three hundred dollars a year, the family was without income.

Not long after he returned home, Daniel recieved a letter from Ezekiel.

"As I was walking down to the office after a letter," the college student wrote, "I happened to find one cent. That is the first money I have had since the second day I returned for this term. It is a fact, Dan, that when I was called on to return a dollar where I owed it, I had to borrow to repay it. And I have borrowed four times since to pay those from whom I borrowed."

Daniel had to write back that neither he nor his father had money to send, but would try to do so the next week if it were possible. He knew that something had to be done soon if Ezekiel were to finish college and if he were to continue his law training. Ever since he had completed Dartmouth it had been his dream to spend time in Boston finishing his preparation to be a lawyer. But that meant money, and everything beyond their daily needs had to be sent to Ezekiel. Only through a miracle would it ever be possible for him to study in Boston.

In the family gathering each evening for prayers, the Websters began to pray for that miracle. A year went by and then a year and a half. Daniel continued to read Mr. Thompson's books. Just enough money came in to keep Ezekiel in school, and Daniel's dream of going to Boston grew fainter and fainter. In addition to their poverty, he was constantly sick, going through struggle with the measles, rheumatism and dreadful headaches which more than once tempted him to quit his studies entirely. He suspected that too much time spent indoors studying contributed to his ills. The necessity of paying for medicine on top of other expenses was irritating.

"Pills and pukes and vivisections and blisterings and all the apparatus for patching up nature's works are what my soul loathes," he wrote to John Porter that winter. "These factitious substitutes are poor, very poor exchanges for the high vigor which those enjoy who can labor upon the earth—upon the business which God originally set us about. When man seeks to avert the curse of living by the sweat of his brow, when he drives himself into offices, close rooms and airless closets, headaches and heartaches and consumptions are his just punishment."

It was not a very pleasant time for him, especially remembering the income which could have been his back in Fryeburg. There was only the dream of Boston to keep him going.

"I believe that some acquaintance in the capital of New England would be very useful to us who expect to plant ourselves down as country lawyers," he wrote to Jeremy in 1803. "But I cannot control my fortune; I must follow wherever circumstances lead. My going to Boston is therefore much more a matter of hope than of probability; unless something like a miracle puts the means in my hands, I shall not budge from here very soon."

When Ezekiel entered his senior year at Dartmouth both of the brothers realized that one of them must have a paying job if the family was to survive.

"One of us must go to work," Ezekiel told him. "I would be happy to take a term off and work as you did when you were in school. But to take time away from study to go and look for work does not seem to be the best use of my time. Why don't you go to Boston in search of employment for one or both of us? In the meantime I will return to Hanover and implore the God of heaven to meet our needs."

So Daniel headed for Boston in February of 1804, down to the family's last cent and in search of a miracle.

Boston at Last

Daniel's trip to Boston in February of 1804 was the beginning of the miracle for which the family had prayed. When he arrived in that city he immediately sought out an old acquaintance from college days, Cyrus Perkins. To his surprise he learned that Perkins was leaving a position as headmaster of a small private school in Short Street to study medicine and he would be willing to recommend Ezekiel to the trustees.

With Perkins' recommendation Ezekiel was hired immediately and began to teach even before he had received his degree from Dartmouth. He in turn began to write long letters back to Salisbury inviting Daniel to return to Boston and look for a place to finish his reading of the law.

"I now have eight scholars in Latin and Greek whom I shall be obliged to dismiss if I cannot have an assistant, and I dare not at present hire one," Ezekiel wrote. "The tuition of these eight scholars will pay for your board. They recite twice in a day, and it will take you about three fourths of an hour to hear them each time. Here, then, you can support yourself by the labor of one hour and a half each day. If you will spend that time in my school daily, I will board you at as genteel a boarding-house as you can wish or the place affords.''

That summer Daniel accepted his brother's invitation to join him in Boston and the miracle continued.

''Now I have to find a lawyer's office in which to read,'' he told Ezekiel after settling in at the boarding-house where his brother was living. ''I know no one in the legal profession here in the city and did not bring any letters of introduction from New Hampshire. But God has brought us both to Boston and I believe He will continue to lead.''

The first several offices Daniel tried were not interested in a country boy without any letters of introduction.

''Why not try the office of Christopher Gore,'' his friend Cyrus suggested one morning. ''He has just returned from England where he served eight years as a commissioner under appointment from President Washington. Before that Washington made him the first United States district attorney for Massachusetts. You couldn't find a better man under whom to study. He has opened a law office in Scollay's building on Tremont Street and has not as yet hired a clerk, to my knowledge.''

''But would he even consent to an interview with a New Hampshire farm boy, much less hire him?''

''There's only one way to find out,'' came the reply. ''I don't know him, but I think we have some mutual acquaintances.''

When the two young men arrived at Mr. Gore's Tremont Street office an hour later they found that the eminent lawyer was the only one there and was indeed willing to visit with them.

"I would like to present for your consideration as clerk my friend from Dartmouth College, Mr. Daniel Webster," Cyrus began. "He is from New Hampshire, has studied law there in the office of Thomas Thompson and has come to Boston to work and not to play. He is most desirous of becoming your pupil and would appreciate it if you would keep your position as clerk open until he can write back for letters of introduction from New Hampshire."

Mr. Gore looked at Daniel. He was just a boy, obviously rustic, with conspicuous black hair and huge eyes, but with a quality in his eyes which the lawyer had come to recognize during his years of experience.

"Come into my office Mr. Weston," he said. "I have some questions I would like to ask you."

Daniel looked around at first to see if there was someone else in the room, then realizing Mr. Gore had simply misunderstood his name, he followed him into an oak-paneled and shelf-lined office. This handsomely fitted room was a far cry from the simple office of Mr. Thompson, and Daniel felt embarrassed to be taking this aristocrat's time. There was no way he would ever consider him for clerk.

"Sit down, Mr. Weston, and tell me about your family."

For the next fifteen minutes they talked, not about his schooling and books he had read, but about his father and brother and the people he had met in Maine and New Hampshire. Feeling that his host was simply being gracious and not wanting to overstay his welcome, Daniel began to excuse himself.

"My young friend," said Mr. Gore as Daniel rose to leave. "You look as though you might be trusted, and trust is one of the most important qualities a man of the bar must possess. You say that you have come to study and not to waste time. I will take you at your

word. Hang up your hat at once, go into the other
room, take your book and sit down to reading it, and
write at your convenience to New Hampshire for your
letters.''

It all happened so suddenly that Daniel read in the
office of Mr. Gore for a week before the lawyer could
remember his last name correctly.

While working for Mr. Gore, Daniel attended
regularly the sessions of the Massachusetts Supreme
Court and the United States Circuit Court. Back in
New Hampshire he had heard judges who were not
educated themselves make fun of lawyers who quoted
from the great classics he had studied in college. But
not here in Boston. The lawyers he heard arguing
cases before these judges were scholars with strong
and powerful minds and this made him study all the
harder from the books in Mr. Gore's library.

One man Daniel particularly enjoyed hearing was
Theophilus Parsons. He was considered the leader of
the Boston bar, had a remarkable knowledge on subjects as different as Greek, astronomy and carpentry,
and possessed the best law library in the United States.
After hearing him in court Daniel would go back to
his room and write down everything he could
remember about him so that he could imitate those
things Mr. Parsons did so well.

''The characteristic endowments of his mind are
strength and shrewdness,'' he wrote. ''Strength, which
enables him to support his cause; shrewdness, by
which he is always ready to report the sallies of his
adversary. He does not address the jury as a
mechanical body to be put in motion by mechanical
means. He appeals to them as men, each having a
mind capable of receiving the ideas on his own.''

Through listening to Mr. Gore and Mr. Parsons
and other great lawyers, Webster became stronger in

his conviction that naturalness in delivery was more effective than the artificial elocution which was popular. He read Sir Francis Bacon's writings on speech, noting particularly his idea that the furtherance of good must always be the purpose of a man's speaking. His earlier view of the law profession as something despised began to change as he saw men using their speaking abilities to accomplish good results.

Christopher Gore was impressed with his young clerk's abilities and introduced him to his friends in Boston society—Senator Samuel Dexter who had been Secretary of the Treasury, Harrison Gray Otis, a well-known orator, and Daniel Davis, the Solicitor-General. Daniel made other friends as well. During a short time substituting for his brother while Ezekiel went back to Dartmouth for graduation he made the acquaintance of a student by the name of Edward Everett who would be his friend all the rest of his life.

After six wonderful months in Boston, Daniel received an exciting letter from his father.

"The clerk of court of common pleas of the county of Hillsborough has just resigned," Ebenezer Webster wrote. "The chief justice of the court, knowing of your study in the law, has requested that I write to offer you the position. It will mean an income of fifteen hundred dollars a year and you will be able to live here at home."

The prospect of making that much money after scraping by for so long seemed too good to be true to Daniel. He knew that his father still owed money for his college education as well as Ezekiel's, and there was a large mortgage on the farm, too. This salary would cover the major portion of those debts and allow him to care for his father comfortably the rest of his life.

Thrilled with the offer, he took the letter to the office to show to Mr. Gore. He was sure the lawyer would congratulate him on landing such a fine position, but instead he found himself receiving some advice he hadn't expected to hear.

"You say that the salary is presently fifteen hundred dollars a year," Gore began slowly. "I have worked with these county courts before and I dare say that the odds are ten to one that when the justices realize the fees have grown so large they will reduce the salary. The time of hiring a new clerk is the logical time to do that, and you must realize it as a possibility. Furthermore, you are appointed now by friends of your father. Others may one day fill their places who have friends of their own to provide for, and even if you were to retain the position, what would you be but a clerk for life."

The words hit Daniel like a bucket of ice water. Here was comfort and even riches within his grasp and he was being asked to reject them for an uncertain future.

"You can be more than a clerk," Mr. Gore continued. "You can be an actor on the stage of life rather than a recorder of other men's actions. Go on, and finish your studies; you are poor enough, but there are greater evils than poverty. Live on no man's favor. What bread you eat, let it be the bread of independence."

What he said made sense to Daniel. In fact, the confidence of his teacher that he could become more than a clerk confirmed in him the feeling he had known during his college days, the feeling that the God who controlled the affairs of men as well as nations had something specific for him to do. But that didn't make it any easier to go back to Salisbury and tell his father that he couldn't accept the job which would solve the money problems the family had faced for years.

Arriving home during a frigid spell in January of 1805, Daniel found his father sitting in front of a fire, looking as old and pale as his son could ever remember him.

As soon as Daniel sat down, he said, "Well, Daniel, we have got that office for you."

Daniel nodded, not certain how to begin. He knew Ebenezer had eyed that position for years, desiring it for him.

"Yes, Father," he said. "The gentlemen were very kind. I must go and thank them."

"They gave it to you without my saying a word about it," Ebenezer smiled. "They know you will do well."

"I must go and see Judge Farrar, and tell him I am much obliged to him," was Daniel's reply as he continued to search for a way to break the bad news to his father.

But Mr. Webster knew his boy much better than Daniel had ever suspected. Straightening himself up in his chair he looked right through him, guessing immediately his reason for the long trip home from Boston.

"Daniel, don't you mean to take that office?"

Daniel looked at his father and then at his mother. She, too, was smiling sadly, anticipating the decision he had made. "No indeed Father," he began slowly, trying to choose the best words, ones which would not hurt those he loved so well. "I want to continue my studies in Mr. Gore's office. It is not that I do not appreciate what you have done, Father. You have always done more for me than I could ever hope to repay. But I do hope to do better than to be a clerk all of my life. I mean to use my tongue in the courts, not my pen; to be an actor, not a register of other men's actions."

The boy rose to his feet, as if pleading his case before his father's court. "I hope yet, sir, to astonish your Honor, in your own court, by my professional attainments."

When he finished he watched closely for the effect his words would have on his father. At first he thought he was angry, but then a look of admiration came over Ebenezer's face. He had always had ambition for Daniel and felt that the position as clerk was the fulfillment of that ambition. But now he was able to see in his son's eyes a vision which far outreached his own. He realized that this son for whom he had sacrificed would one day plead a case, not only in court on which he sat, but in many other courtrooms as well, perhaps even before the Supreme Court of the United States.

"Well, my son," he said, with pride gleaming from his eyes in spite of the disappointment, "your mother has always said you would come to something or nothing, she was not sure which. I think you are now about settling that doubt for her."

Back in Boston Daniel applied himself once more to his reading and two months later, on the motion of Christopher Gore, was admitted to practice in the court of common pleas in Boston.

Now Daniel could be a lawyer on his own, not a clerk for somebody else. He wanted to move to Portsmouth where he thought he could prosper as a lawyer, but his father's health was declining rapidly so he decided to settle closer to home and care for his parents in their old age. Thus it was that he opened an office in Boscawen, where he had gone ten years earlier to study with Dr. Wood.

Daniel began to represent clients in Boscawen in surrounding towns as well. From the start he made a strong impression in the courts, and soon he had the privilege of arguing a case before the court of common pleas where Judge Ebenezer Webster was sitting.

Living in Boscawen meant Daniel was close enough to worship in his old church, the Congregational Church of Salisbury, where Thomas Worcester was now pastor. Realizing he had neglected his spiritual life during his time in Boston, he resolved to be regular in his attendance now that he was near his home church. The first Sunday back he saw there might be an additional reason for church attendance as well.

"It's so good to see you again, Daniel," Rev. Worcester greeted him after the service. "Allow me to introduce you to some other young people who have recently moved here."

That was exactly what the young lawyer was hoping to hear. He had noticed before the service the arrival on horseback of an "angel" in a black velvet dress. It was a face he had not seen before in Salisbury.

"Mr. Webster, this is Miss Grace Fletcher. Miss Fletcher, Mr. Daniel Webster."

Daniel bowed his best bow from Boston social days and followed it with a gallant attempt at interesting conversation. He discovered that Miss Fletcher was a minister's daughter from Hopkinton who was living with a married sister in Salisbury. She had just completed a term of teaching school. Unlike the girls at Hanover, she had read many of the same books Daniel enjoyed and was able to talk about them intelligently.

Pleased, Daniel went home eager to return for the next church service. Grace and her cousin rode back to the farm laughing about the awkward boy who had talked to them so long after church. They were not impressed.

We the People...

8

Big-City Lawyer

Daniel Webster's visits to church were almost the only social activity he had during the next two years in Boscawen. Judge Webster was very ill. In fact, the case his son argued before him was the last time he heard Daniel in court. Starting a new law practice was hard work, and Daniel kept busy night and day to earn enough to support himself and his parents. Seeing Grace Fletcher from week to week in church helped, although there was never enough time or money to court her the way he wanted to.

In addition to going to church to see Grace, Daniel found that for the first time since boyhood he was thinking about God and about his beliefs. The minister, Thomas Worcester, encouraged Daniel in his thinking, stopping in many times at his law office to discuss the Scriptures and what they taught. His sermons were long and consisted primarily of lists of reasons why he believed the doctrines of the Word of God. This appealed to Webster, who thought that all speaking should be logical argumentation. Along with his work and continuing studies he began to draw up his own list of what he believed.

Webster approached the Word of God in the same manner in which he had approached his other studies. He had read the Bible and memorized portions of it since he was small. Several years earlier he had translated the entire New Testament from the Greek. Now he set about in a systematic fashion to see what it taught on definite subjects. He had always believed that God was in control of the universe, but he wanted to be certain that such was actually the teaching of the Bible. He believed that Jesus Christ was divine, that He was the Son of God. He had learned that in church and he had accepted it. Now he wanted to see proof for that belief in God's Word. He had accepted the authority of the Scriptures themselves, believed that they were the Word of God. Now he wanted to prove to his own satisfaction that he had not been misled. He wanted to search out the Scriptures for himself in order to know for certain that they were what he had always believed them to be.

Though Grace had laughed about Daniel's "awkwardness" the first day she met him, her view of him began to change. Her sister's husband and others in the community spoke highly of Daniel, telling her that they believed him to be a man of great promise. His reputation as a lawyer was becoming well-known throughout the community. However, it was his regular church attendance and his study of the Word of God which impressed her far more than his fame. As the daughter of a clergyman, Grace had always been regular in church attendance herself and felt that it was important. She would not seriously consider any young man who did not go to church. But religion to Grace Fletcher was more than a matter of church attendance. As a young girl, she had accepted

Christ as the One who provided for her salvation through his death on the cross. She was confident of her salvation and wanted to be sure that her marriage, should it ever come about, would be centered in the person of Christ, as her life already was.

In a letter to a friend she wrote, "Such is our stupidity that we neglect the all important realities of eternity for the trifling follies of this vain, delusive world, and scarce a thought aspires to heaven. Let us rouse from our stupor, and oh! may we be prepared for the momentous period which surely awaits us." Her first concern was how to please her Maker.

Starting a new law office in a small New Hampshire town involved primarily the writing of legal documents such as writs and summonses for a dollar apiece. As this did not require knowledge of the classics and literature which Daniel loved so much, he soon became bored with the work. But he was determined to stay close to home in order to care for his parents. One way he sought to relieve the boredom was through letter writing. He wrote to his old friend Jeremy Bingham a letter in which he joked about his job by putting one of the summonses into poetry.

> "All good sheriffs in the land
>   We command
> That forthwith you arrest John Dyer
>   Esquire
> If in your precinct you can find him
>   and bind him."

In April, 1806, Daniel came home from the law office one evening to find his father's condition much worse. Sitting down by the judge's bed he talked of hunting and fishing, of Ezekiel and the rest of the family until finally, worn out from a life of exertion and hard work, Ebenezer Webster closed his eyes and died. After the funeral Daniel and Ezekiel discussed the future, now that their father was gone.

"One of us must care for the farm and for mother," Daniel said. "We are all she has now that father is gone."

"I know you don't care about farming," Ezekiel answered. "But if you would keep things together until I can finish reading for my law examination, perhaps I can move back here from Boston."

"Would you be willing to do that? You know I wanted to settle in Portsmouth a year ago but knew I was needed here. If you would come to Boscawen you could take my business here and watch over the farm and mother. For my part, I would assume the responsibility for the debt on Elms Farm and contribute to mother's care as well."

So it was settled that Ezekiel would return to Boston to finish reading for the law and Daniel would remain in Salisbury until that time. The anticipation of a move to a larger community excited Daniel. He looked forward to the greater opportunity in the courts which the move to Portsmouth would provide. But there were still two matters which had to be cared for before he left his hometown.

The first concerned church membership. Although he had been baptized in the Congregational church in Salisbury when he was younger, he had never formally united with the church. Convinced from his studies that his doctrinal beliefs agreed with the Word of God and with the preaching of Thomas Worcester, he desired to take the step of church membership as a witness to the community concerning what he believed.

With this purpose in mind he finished writing down his list of doctrines of the Christian faith. He defended logically from the Scriptures the providence of God,

the divinity of Christ and the authority of the Scrip-
ture. These he gave to Rev. Worcester along with his
request to be considered for church membership.
Worcester was pleased with the spiritual growth he
had seen in Webster since his return to Salisbury and
by his recommendation he was accepted as a member
of the Congregational church of Salisbury on August
8, 1807.

Ezekiel returned from Boston about the same time
and Daniel found himself continuing his courtship of
Grace Fletcher by letter from the city of Portsmouth.
She was pleased that he had joined the church and
was now writing to him regularly.

The move to Portsmouth marked a great change
in Daniel Webster's career as a lawyer. Though he
had impressed the farm people and the other lawyers
in the valleys of western New Hampshire he had not
faced the well-trained men who were defending clients
in the more populous parts of the state. In Boscawen
and Salisbury he had been the most eloquent man
around, but such was not the case in Portsmouth.

During one of his first cases in Portsmouth he found
himself opposed by Senator William Plumer, one of
the best lawyers in the state. Mr. Plumer quoted some
lines from a book called *Peake's Law of Evidence*, which
Webster did not think compared to the best law books
he had read.

"The Honorable Mr. Plumer has chosen to quote
from Peake," he declaimed when it was his turn to
speak. "But Peake is a ridiculous compilation of bad
laws, a book which should not even be admissable in
a courtroom in New Hampshire."

Then in a dramatic fashion, which had served him
well back in Boscawen he picked up the book in question and threw it down on the table in front of him.
"So much for Mr. Thomas Peake's compendium of
the Law of Evidence."

Daniel thought he had destroyed Senator Plumer's entire argument. When he used such emotional speeches back in the valley people had cheered, and opposing lawyers had been silenced out of embarrassment for their lack of education. But Senator Plumer was not embarrassed, nor was he silent.

Rising to his feet once again he stared at the young man across the table from him and then turned to the jury. "I appreciate the young man's opinion of Peake, but we must remember that it is just that, an opinion. Allow me to read this same opinion from one I trust Mr. Webster will respect."

Quietly the lawyer began to read the same quotation from a volume of court reports he had beside him. When he finished he addressed the entire court in general and Daniel Webster in particular. "That, my friends, was the same opinion we just heard from the much despised Peake. In fact, it was the quotation recently used from Mr. Peake. The source this time was Lord Mansfield himself in one of his most famous decisions. Perhaps Mr. Webster would care to enlighten us concerning the opinion Lord Mansfield held of Mr. Peake's book."

From that experience and others, Daniel realized that he had much to learn and he took as his prime example the greatest of all the New England lawyers, Jeremiah Mason.

Mason was impressive in the courtroom, six feet seven inches tall, with a frame to match. The first time Daniel argued against Mason in court he was replacing the state's attorney who had suddenly become ill. Mason was defending one of Portsmouth's leading citizens who was accused of passing counterfeit money.

Daniel made a great speech which the jury enjoyed so much that he wasn't concerned at all when he heard

Mason shuffle up close to the jury box and start to
talk with the jurors in a conversational manner. There
was no way Mason's client could avoid a guilty verdict, Daniel was sure. But to his amazement the jury
found him not guilty.

"He had a habit," Daniel said, "of standing quite
near to the jury, so near that he might have laid his
finger on the foreman's nose; and then he talked to
them in a plain conversational way, in short sentences,
and using no word that was not level to the com-
prehension of the least educated man on the panel."

Listening to Mr. Mason, Daniel soon realized that
his quotations from the classics might be impressive
in Fourth of July orations, but they did not impress
members of a jury. He began to simplify his language
and use facts and logic to reason with the jury instead
of trying to impress them with references to Milton
and Cicero. To his delight he began to win more of
his cases, even beating Mason himself from time to
time.

One great advantage Webster had over even the
greatest of the New Hampshire lawyers was his
memory. He never forgot a point of law once he
learned it. He could recall small details of legal decisions from years before and quote them word for word
in the middle of his speeches without ever going back
to check them. He could also use stories from his days
growing up on the farm to charm the country juries
he often faced.

When a witness for his opponent testified that he
had heard a certain statement about "a hundred
times," Daniel rose slowly to his feet and began to
tell a story, almost as if he was thinking about
something else entirely.

"That reminds me of a story I heard about a
hunter. Seems this fellow had been out hunting snakes

and came back telling about how he had seen one hundred black snakes. Each snake was twenty feet long and they were all lined up in a row. Well, some of his friends thought he was exaggerating just a mite. So he told the story again, except this time there were only fifty black snakes, still twenty feet long and lined up in a row. Some of his friends were still skeptical so he decided there were perhaps only ten snakes. Finally the hunter got down to two and that was where he took his stand. 'I won't give up another snake', he said. 'I'll give up the story first.' ''

While the jury and the entire courtroom was laughing at the story, Daniel made his point. "If my friend on the witness stand would remember that story of the hunter perhaps he would give up his story before he gave up another snake."

Jeremiah Mason and the other lawyers soon came to respect the newcomer's talent and he and Daniel became good friends. After hearing him many times in the courtroom as well as listening to him read the great speeches of Hamlet, Othello and Macbeth in the privacy of his own home, Mason declared that the stage had lost a great actor when Daniel decided to enter the field of law.

Not wanting to lose the spiritual progress he had made in Salisbury, Daniel began to attend the Congregational church in Portsmouth. The minister was Dr. Buckminster, the father of one of his tutors from Exeter. Buckminster not only took the responsibility for his spiritual training, but also, seeing that he was still quite frail, encouraged him to exercise each morning by sawing wood for half an hour. Often this was done behind the parsonage with Daniel on one end of a cross-cut saw and the preacher on the other end. Then they joined the family for breakfast, something which pleased the minister's daughter. She thought Daniel extremely attractive and a remarkable person.

Although the opportunities for courtship were greater in Portsmouth, Daniel could not forget Grace Fletcher. On a visit home in the spring of 1808 she accepted his proposal of marriage, and Rev. Worcester performed the ceremony in the Congregational church in Salisbury on June 24. The couple traveled back to Portsmouth to a home Webster had purchased not far from his office on Market Square.

With the exercise and Grace's cooking, Daniel began to fill out his frame to match the large head he had always possessed. After twenty-five years of poor health he developed a strong constitution for which he gave all of the credit to God. His appearance in court was enough to impress any judge. One reporter in Grafton, New Hampshire, described seeing Daniel and Ezekiel arrive for a case they were sharing in these words: "I can see them now, driving into that little village in their billows-top chaise—top thrown back—driving like Jehu, the chaise bending under them like a close-top in a high wind. I could have told either of them thirty miles among a thousand men."

Daniel's fame in the courtroom did not go unnoticed back in Hanover. The trustees of Dartmouth College invited him to give the Phi Beta Kappa address at the college in the summer of 1809. He and Grace, accompanied by the Jeremiah Masons, made the trip across the hills to do so.

Daniel chose to speak on "The State of our Literature" and warned the students that there were two obstacles to literary improvement. The first was the love of money, "a mean, monkish, idolatrous devotion to it, which when once enthroned in the heart, banishes thence every generous sentiment."

The second obstacle was the pursuit of politics, "the mad strife of temporary parties, the rancor of conflicting interests and jarring opinions. These are vials of wrath the contents of which scorch and consume all that is desirable and lovely in society."

It was appropriate for him to discuss the dangers of politics for already he was becoming one of the leaders of the Federalist party in New Hampshire. All too soon he would be faced with the difficulty of pursuing politics while avoiding the mad strife which so often accompanied it.

The War of 1812

War! The drums and marching feet which had thrilled young Daniel in the stories his father told of the Revolutionary War came once again to the United States. This time, however, Webster was not sure the fighting was necessary.

It had been brewing for some time. Ever since taking office in 1801, President Thomas Jefferson found himself caught between the British and the French armies which were fighting in Europe. Many of Daniel's friends in New England were merchants and shipowners whose business was selling goods and carrying goods back and forth between Europe and America by boat. American ships traveling to or from France were being captured by the British navy, and those traveling to or from Great Britain were being captured by the French navy. In addition to stopping these ships, the British often took the crewmen, claiming they were deserters from the Royal Army.

Merchants and shipowners of New England wanted the President to build a larger and stronger navy to protect their trade. Farmers of the South and West didn't care about the trade, but they were upset with the British for pressing American men into service in the Royal Navy. President Jefferson's solution to the problem was to keep all American ships at home. To do this he asked Congress to pass an embargo bill which prohibited trade with either France or Great Britain. This satisfied the South and West but angered New Englanders because they were losing business by keeping their ships in port.

The embargo caused many problems in Portsmouth. Merchants there turned from being angry with the British and French to being angry with the President. Since they were Federalists and Jefferson was a Democratic-Republican they felt that their problems were a result of the way he was running the country. Daniel saw idle seamen, dismantled ships, grass growing on the wharves, closed warehouses and ruined merchants. In response to requests from friends he wrote a strong pamphlet in favor of repealing the embargo.

Because of the pressure from New England the embargo was repealed just before President Jefferson left office. His successor, President James Madison, was also a Democratic-Republican, however, and he continued the previous administration's policies toward England. Farmers in the South and West were facing hostile Indians and were certain that British forces in Canada and Florida were behind the trouble. This gave them a new reason to call for war against England.

The pressure on President Madison to declare war on England was led by John C. Calhoun, a representative from South Carolina, and Henry Clay, a representative from Kentucky. These two men soon became known as "War Hawks" because they wanted to go to war with England in order to remove the border Indian menace and allow the farmers in the South and West to acquire more land. Their idea was to annex Florida and Canada and make them a part of the United States.

On November 7, 1811, Indians in the Ohio Valley made a surprise attack on General William Henry Harrison's troops. Although Harrison lost 185 men out of 6,000 he defeated the Indians. When word of this victory arrived in Washington the War Hawks hailed it as the victory of the Battle of Tippecanoe and renewed their calls for a declaration of war.

By the following summer President Madison was convinced that there was no way to get England to agree to quit capturing our ships and encouraging the Indians short of going to war against them. He asked Congress to declare war and they agreed to do so on June 18, 1812. The vote was very close. The Federalists, particularly those from New England, voted against declaring war.

Back in Portsmouth, Daniel Webster continued his work as a lawyer, watching closely what was going on in Washington. He never forgot the day his father told him about the man who was a representative because he was college educated while Judge Webster was not in Congress because he had not received an education. Daniel had his education now and was waiting for an opportunity to use it.

On July 4, 1812, just three weeks after Congress declared war, Daniel Webster spoke before the Portsmouth chapter of the Washington Benevolent Society. In his speech he argued that since the abuses of the British had come at sea we should fight them at sea and not on land. He insisted that the nation should abandon any thought of invading Canada and that the President's first responsibility should be to bring the conflict to an early and honorable close.

Many in New England at that time were willing to separate from the southern and western states because of their anger and bitterness over the policies of Jefferson and Madison. To them Daniel said, "With respect to the war in which we are now involved, the course which our principles requires us to pursue cannot be doubtful. It is now the law of the land, and as such we are bound to regard it." He believed so strongly in the Constitution that he could not justify rebellion against it even in the present case. However, he made it clear that they should use every legal method to restore sense to the national government. "At the same time the world may be assured that we know our rights and shall exercise them. We shall express our opinions on this, as on every measure of the government. By the exercise of our constitutional right of suffrage, by the peaceable remedy of election, we shall seek to restore wisdom to our councils, and peace to our country."

This speech to the Washington Benevolent Society was printed and copies were distributed throughout New Hampshire. A convention of the people was held in Rockingham the next August, and Daniel was a delegate from the city of Portsmouth. There he addressed the more than two thousand representatives who gathered to protest the war and held them spellbound with a ninety-minute speech.

Following the speeches seventeen men were chosen to write a resolution to President Madison informing him of their views. Webster was one of those seventeen. They wrote the resolution in the form of an oration addressed to the President. It reviewed the course of events leading up to the war, explained the opposition of the Federalists of New England, urged a vigorous naval defense and warned the President against any alliance with Napoleon.

People who heard Webster speak at the Rockingham Convention were so impressed that they
nominated him for Congress as representative of the
state of New Hampshire. In November of 1812 he
was elected to the House of Representatives.

When the new session of Congress began in May
of 1813, Daniel was only thirty-one years old. He and
Grace had one daughter named Grace. Since Mrs.
Webster was expecting another child she remained in
Portsmouth while Daniel went to Washington alone.
The City of Washington was new, not as nice a place
to live as Portsmouth. After Daniel arrived and settled
into a boardinghouse, he wrote his first impressions
of his journey.

"From Baltimore to this place, the whole distance,
almost, you travel through woods and on a worse road
than you ever saw. There are two or three plantations
looking tolerably well—all the rest is desert."

His impression of the city itself was even worse. He
was shocked by its emptiness. Five miles of scattered
shacks and houses were interrupted only by woods and
gravel pits. The distance between the main government buildings were so great that on at least one
occasion a party of congressmen got lost within a mile
of the Capitol and spent the entire night wandering
through gullies, thickets and swamps. There were
grizzly bears penned up in front of the president's
mansion and the slave market was one of the busiest
places in the city. New Hampshire had abolished
slavery when Daniel was one year old and it was a
great shock to see men and women being bought and
sold within a mile of the capitol.

In spite of the condition of Washington as a city,
Daniel discovered old friends and made new ones as
well. Christopher Gore of Boston was now a Senator
and lived at the same boardinghouse where Webster

resided. Jeremiah Mason joined them as the newly elected senator from Hew Hampshire. Other Federalists lived in the house; the custom was to board with others of similar political views who came from the same part of the country. The War Hawks lived at a different boardinghouse.

Henry Clay, the leader of the War Hawks, was from Hanover County, Virginia, near the home of Patrick Henry. As a boy he had heard the great patriot speak and had taken him as his model. While serving in the office of George Wythe and studying law under Robert Brooke he paid special attention to developing his oratory. He joined the Richmond debating society and sharpened his skills by arguing cases against other young lawyers of the city. When he was ready to practice law he left Virginia and moved to Lexington, Kentucky, a flourishing frontier town. Here he advanced rapidly in both law and politics. By the time Webster arrived in Washington, Henry Clay had been there for seven years and was serving as speaker of the House of Representatives. Clay was a natural orator who spoke rapidly, pouring out words so quickly that he overwhelmed his listeners. As a leader of the War Hawks he was firmly committed to a military victory over England.

John C. Calhoun was Clay's chief supporter. He was born in the same year as Webster, but far to the south, on the South Carolina frontier. His father, like Daniel's, was a tough Scotch-Irishman who had grown up fighting Indians. John attended Yale, where he was a member of the debating club, and then entered the law profession. He had been a representative since 1810 and was already recognized as one of the most influential voices in Congress. He was chairman of the Committee on Foreign Relations which was directly in charge of legislation concerning war.

Calhoun represented the South's point of view while Clay represented the West's. John Calhoun always dressed in black, with his long hair brushed straight back from his high forehead and his gray-yellow eyes riveting his listeners. He was a poor speaker, but he commanded attention anyway because of his great logic and choice of words.

Daniel Webster's strong opposition to the war soon brought him to the attention of Henry Clay and John Calhoun. They recognized in him an opponent who was equal to them in oratory. After the summer break Daniel returned from Portsmouth to find that he had been dropped from the Foreign Relations Committee.

In the House of Representatives he began to deliver speeches which would change the course of the nation over the next forty years. Early in 1814 he spoke against a bill to encourage men to enlist in the army. Although he was willing to fight if he believed it was necessary, he was keeping his promise to the people of New Hampshire to use whatever legal means were available to bring the war to a conclusion. The speech was reprinted in Federalist newspapers, whose editors were excited to find a man on their side who could speak as well as Clay and Calhoun.

"Mr. Madison's" war with England, as the Federalists called it, was not going well for the United States at all. An attempt to invade Canada had failed. British troops landed on the coast of Maine and threatened to invade all of New England. Back in Portsmouth for spring recess, Daniel was chosen chairman of the local committee for defense. He immediately summoned all able-bodied men to assemble with their guns on the parade grounds. He had stated that he was willing to defend his home if necessary and he was ready to prove that statement. Before the militia could leave for battle, however, word came that the British had retired from the shore of Maine.

In the meantime the city of Washington did not escape the war. The British fleet in Chesapeake Bay launched a raid on the nation's capital which left most of the government buildings in ruin. The executive mansion was burned and President Madison and his family fled for their lives.

Returning to Washington following his reelection to a second term in the House, Daniel was even more determined to fight against continuing the war which many people felt had become a hopeless cause. He spoke against a bill that would have permitted the national army to draft soldiers instead of waiting for them to volunteer. His argument was that it was the right of the states to raise their own militia. "It is the solemn duty of the State Governments to protect their own authority over their own militia, and to interpose between their citizens and arbitrary power."

The Governors of Connecticut and Massachusetts had already refused to permit their state militia to leave those states in order to invade Canada. General Hull surrendered his forces to the British in Detroit. Indians led by British officers slaughtered American troops at Fort Dearborn and Van Rensselaer's army suffered a crushing defeat on the Canadian side of the Niagara. Only in sea battles did the Americans gain any victories. President Madison felt strongly that he must draft soldiers from the state militias. But Daniel felt just as strongly that it was not the right thing to do.

This speech was one of the best Webster had given. It looked as if the Federalist viewpoint on the war was becoming more popular. Many were predicting that if the war did not end soon the Madison presidency would be destroyed.

Early in January, 1815, General Andrew Jackson's riflemen defeated a highly trained British army of five

thousand men in the Battle of New Orleans. Jackson
lost only sixty-three Americans while killing almost
two thousand redcoats. When word of the victory
reached Washington the city exploded with a great
celebration. Torchlight parades were held in the streets
which not long before had seen the torches of the
British army.

The country was still celebrating this victory when
word arrived that a treaty was signed with the British
in the city of Ghent. As it turned out, the treaty had
been signed before the battle of New Orleans, making the battle unnecessary. But the nation felt that they
had defeated the British army for a second time, and
Andrew Jackson was a hero. The Federalists who had
opposed the war were considered traitors, not much
better than Benedict Arnold. Although he had stood
for the Constitution and what he thought was right,
Daniel Webster was considered by many to be disloyal
to his country.

Webster faced other problems as well that made him
wonder if it was worth his time to stay in Washington.
His house in Portsmouth burned down and Grace and
the children barely escaped with their lives. Everything
else was lost. His library was destroyed and his house,
worth six thousand dollars, was not insured. The fire
left him deeply in debt.

"This life, though great, does not much move me
when I reflect on the dangers my family were in,"
he wrote to a friend. It was not easy being away from
his family for such long periods of time. He seriously
considered resigning from his position in Washington
and returning to the practice of law.

With that purpose in mind he moved his family to
Boston where he felt there would be better opportunity
to make a living as a lawyer. There was one session
left in his term in Congress. In November of 1816

he talked Grace into leaving little Grace and her brother Daniel in Boston with friends while she went with him to Washington. She had never seen the capital and was excited about meeting Daniel's friends in Washington, seeing the damage the British had done during the war, and meeting the President.

In the middle of the term, word came from Boston that six-year-old Grace was ill. Abandoning his duties in the capital, Webster climbed into a coach with Grace and drove nonstop night and day to Boston.

When they arrived they were told that Grace was dying of tuberculosis. It was too late to do anything to save her life. Daniel sat by her bed, reading to her for hours and telling her stories to make her laugh. The great voice which had moved crowds of people was completely occupied with helping one little girl.

When she slept restlessly, Daniel and his wife prayed for her, asking God for a miracle. But it was not to be. One evening, a week later, Gracie looked up adoringly at her father and closed her eyes for the last time.

Turning away from the bed, Daniel Webster stood with tears running down his cheeks. For most of his little girl's life he had been in Washington serving his country. It didn't seem then as if anyone appreciated his work. He was discouraged with political life and determined never to return to Washington.

America's Greatest Speech

In order to get over the death of Gracie, Daniel worked even harder to set up his business as a lawyer in Boston than he had been working as a congressman in Washington. Many large manufacturing firms and shipping firms in the city were interested in having him represent them. Within the first month he was collecting fees for court appearances which were as much as he had made in a year in Portsmouth.

But there were great expenses as well. The family bought a house at the summit of Beacon Hill, on Mount Vernon Street, a four-story structure large enough for his growing family. Daniel Fletcher, their oldest boy was soon joined by Julia, Edward and baby Charlie. They often entertained their new friends in Boston and sometimes guests from Europe as well. On one occasion they had a formal candlelight reception for the grear Revolutionary War hero Lafayette. Though Daniel was making more money than he ever had before, it seemed that there was never enough. So Daniel accepted more responsibilities, doing the work of three or four ordinary men.

Even though he was extremely busy, he determined not to miss the time with these children which he had missed with Gracie when he was away at Washington. Every evening after dinner he carried into the living room the book he was currently reading and seated himself on the couch. Edward and Charlie climbed over him and the couch as he read, pretending he was a mountain. Julie and Fletcher sat close by on the floor, reading as well, while Mrs. Webster knitted in her chair.

In the morning Daniel was the first to rise. He woke up the rest of the household by singing hymns at the top of his lungs. Many of them were the old William Cowper hymns he had memorized as a boy.

> *"Ye sons of earth prepare the plough*
> *Break up your fallow ground;*
> *The sower is gone forth to sow*
> *And scatter blessings round.*
>
> *The seed that finds a stony soil*
> *Shoots forth a hasty blade;*
> *But ill repays the sower's toil,*
> *Soon withered, scorched and dead.*
>
> *The thorny ground is sure to balk*
> *All hopes of harvest there;*
> *We find a tall and sickly stalk*
> *But not the fruitful ear.*
>
> *The beaten path and highway side,*
> *Receive the trust in vain;*
> *The watchful birds the spoil divide,*
> *And pick up all the grain.*
>
> *But where the Lord of grace and power*
> *Has blessed the happy field,*

How plenteous is the golden store
   The deep-wrought furrows yield!

Father of mercies, we have need
   Of thy preparing grace;
Let the same Hand that gives the seed
   Provide a fruitful place!

After the entire family was roused Daniel set off for his morning horseback ride dressed in a frock coat, with tight pantaloons, and a pair of blucher boots reaching to the knee and adorned with a tassel. On one side of the head was a bell-crowned beaver hat and in his hand a riding whip. By the time he returned, breakfast was ready and the day had begun. The children remembered those years in Boston as some of the happiest of their lives.

Daniel's work sometimes took him back to Washington even though he was no longer serving in Congress. His work was now as a lawyer before the Supreme Court of the United States.

One of the first cases he argued before the Supreme Court involved Dartmouth, the college he had attended. Dartmouth College was a private institution which operated under a royal charter granted by the colonial governor of New Hampshire to Eleazar Wheelock in 1769. The charter designated that the college be run by Wheelock and a board of trustees who could choose their own members.

In 1779 President Wheelock was succeeded by his son John who was president of Dartmouth when Daniel was a student. After he had been president for almost twenty years a problem arose between him and some of the trustees of the college. In a college board meeting they voted to replace him as president with a man named Francis Brown.

John Wheelock, feeling that Dartmouth had been taken away from him unfairly, appealed to the governor of New Hampshire for help. The governor convinced the legislature to revise the college charter, changing the name to Dartmouth University and appointing a new group of trustees. The new trustees reelected Wheelock to the presidency and now there were two boards and two presidents both trying to run the same college. The entire argument was then taken into the courts.

President Wheelock asked Webster to take the case on behalf of the legislature and the new trustees, but instead he chose to join his old friends Thomas Thompson and Jeremiah Mason on the side of the original trustees. Since the governor of the state had appointed the judges who heard the case, they decided in favor of one of the new trustees and the case moved on to the Supreme Court.

The Supreme Court building was not yet completed in Washington, so the court met in a basement room in one of the other buldings. On most days they met with few visitors, but when word got around that Webster or William Wirt, the attorney general, or some other popular speaker was addressing the court it was difficult to find an empty seat.

The Chief Justice of the Supreme Court was John Marshall. Marshall had been raised in a frontier log cabin, had taught himself by reading Pope's *Essay on Man* and other books just as Webster did when he was a boy. He had been with Washington at Valley Forge as a Revolutionary soldier before becoming a lawyer and politician. He was also a Federalist and a strong leader. His arguments were often enough to convince the rest of the judges to decide his way.

The Dartmouth case came before the Supreme Court on March 10, 1818. Webster was the first to speak and began to talk with the judges in a tone of easy yet dignified conversation.

"The general question is, whether the acts of the legislature of New Hampshire of the 27th of June, and of the 18th and 26th of December, 1816, are valid and binding on the plaintiffs, without their acceptance or assent."

He then proceeded to explain the background of the case, telling how Eleazar Wheelock had started the school on his own plantation, at his own expense. He recounted how, in the early years of the school Mr. Wheelock had "clothed, maintained and educated a number of native Indians, and employed them afterwards as missionaries and schoolmasters among the savage tribes."

Still speaking in a conversational manner he told the justices how the Earl of Dartmouth had contributed money to the school, causing Mr. Wheelock to give it it's name, and how the King in 1769 had granted Dartmouth College a royal charter.

After reviewing the history of the case without even looking at the papers in front of him, Webster's voice grew stronger. "After the institution thus created and constituted had existed, uninterruptedly and usefully, nearly fifty years, the legislature of New Hampshire passed the acts in question."

For the next four hours, like a lion at bay, Daniel argued before the justices. He claimed that the charter granted to Mr. Wheelock had created a private and not a public corporation and therefore the legislature did not have the right as a public body to change that charter. He said that the charter was between the one who had granted it and the trustees to whom it had been granted and not between the state of New Hampshire and the trustees. Then, almost as an afterthought, he used the argument which was to decide the case and make this speech one of the most famous speeches in American history. He argued that "the acts in question are repugnant to the tenth section of the first article of the Constitution of the United States."

Remembering back all the way to when he had purchased that handkerchief and read the Constitution for the first time, Webster quoted the article. *No state shall pass any bill of attainder, ex post facto law, or law impairing the obligation of contracts.*

On the basis of the Constitution, Webster claimed that New Hampshire did not have the right to change the contract of a private college. "The case before the court is not of ordinary importance, nor of everyday occurrence," he said. "It affects not this college only, but every college, and all the literary institutions of the country. They have all a common principle of existence, the inviolability of their charters."

"But it is more. It is, in some sense, the case of every man who has property of which he may be stripped, for the question is simply this: shall our state legislature be allowed to take that which is not their own, to turn it from its original use, and apply it to such ends or purposes as they, in their discretion, shall see fit?"

For a moment it seemed as if he was finished. The long pause brought all movement in the crowded room to a stop. Daniel walked slowly to the very center of the little room and stopped in front of the chief justice. With a catch in his voice, as if he were having a hard time keeping back the tears, he spoke directly to Justice John Marshall.

"Sir, you may destroy this little institution; it is weak, it is in your hands! You may put it out; but if you do, you must carry on your work! You must extinguish, one after another, all those great lights of science, which, for more than a century, have thrown their radiance over the land! It is, sir, as I have said, a small college—and yet there are those who love it!"

Then his voice did break and several of the justices were seen to be wiping away tears as well. When he was finally able to continue he brought his speech to a dramatic finish.

"Sir, I know not how others may feel, but, for myself, when I see my alma mater surrounded, like Caesar in the senate house, by those who are reiterating stab upon stab, I would not, for this right hand, have her turn to me and say, 'and thou too, my son.' "

For two more days the court continued to hear arguments from the other lawyers and then they adjourned their session without making a decision. It was not until the following year that the decision was announced. Daniel Webster had won his greatest case yet before the Supreme Court.

Webster's speech before the Supreme Court was never printed in its entirety. But two years later he gave a speech which has been printed in school textbooks and memorized by young people ever since that time. It happened on December 22, 1820. He was asked to give a speech in Plymouth, Massachusetts, in honor of the Pilgrims who had landed there two hundred years before.

An old friend George Ticknor was one of the twelve hundred people who crowded into First Church to hear him speak. After listening to Webster for two hours, George wrote to a friend that he "was never so excited by public speaking before in my life. Three or four times I thought my temples would burst with the gush of blood; for, after all, you must know that I am aware that it is no connected and compacted whole, but a collection of wonderful fragments of burning eloquence, to which his whole manner gave tenfold force. It seemed to me as if he was like the mount that might not be touched and that burned with fire."

In preparing his Plymouth Oration, Daniel went

back to his own religious upbringing and remembered how God had been good not only to him, but to the entire nation as well.

"Let us rejoice that we behold this day," he told those gathered at First Church of Plymouth. "Let us be thankful that we have lived to see the bright and happy breaking of the auspicious morn, which commences the third century of the history of New England. Auspicious indeed, bringing a happiness beyond the common allotment of Providence to men."

Before beginning his story of the early Pilgrims he summarized all of history, "which begins with the origin of our race, runs onward through its successive generations, binding together the past, the present, and the future, and terminating at last, with the consummation of all things earthly, at the throne of God." There was no doubt in Webster's mind where all of them would stand when life was over.

Then, putting words into the mouths of those who landed on Plymouth rock he told the familiar story, emphasizing the reason for which they made the difficult journey—religious freedom.

"If God shall prosper us," Daniel claimed the first pilgrims might well have said, "If God shall prosper us, we shall here begin a work which shall last for ages; we shall plant here a new society, in the principles of the fullest liberty and the purest religion; we shall subdue this wilderness which is before us; we shall fill this region of the great continent which stretches from pole to pole, with civilization and Christianity; the temples of the true God shall rise, where now ascends the smoke of idolatrous sacrifice.''

The major portion of the speech involved a comparison of the American culture with the best days of Greek and Roman culture and a recounting of the history of the last two hundred years. But then Webster turned to some of the benefits New England was enjoying as a result of her history. He praised the Constitution which secured for them the blessings of liberty. He spoke fervently about the schools and colleges which had been started to educate the young. Then he returned again to the blessings of God.

''Lastly, our ancestors established their system of government on morality and religious sentiment. Whatever makes men good Christians, makes them good citizens. Our fathers came here to enjoy their religion free and unmolested; and, at the end of two centuries, there is nothing upon which we can pronounce more confidently, nothing of which we can express a more deep and earnest conviction, than of the inestimable importance of that religion to man, both in regard to this life and that which is to come. Let us cherish these sentiments, and extend this influence still more widely; in the full conviction, that that is the happiest society which partakes in the highest degree of the mild and peaceful spirit of Christianity.''

At the very end of his speech that day Daniel brought up a subject which some people felt did not have a place in a speech about the Pilgrims. That was the matter of slavery. The Missouri Compromise had been passed in Congress that year which admitted

Missouri as a slave state and Maine as a free state. This spread of slavery to new states being carved out of the Louisiana Purchase bothered Webster greatly, and he felt it was perfectly appropriate in a speech concerning his nation and the freedom it enjoyed to mention how he felt about slavery.

"I deem it my duty on this occasion to suggest, that the land is not yet wholly free from the contamination of a traffic, at which every feeling of humanity must forever revolt. I mean the African slave trade. Neither public sentiment, nor the law, has hitherto been able entirely to put an end to this odious and abominable trade.

"It is not fit that the land of the Pilgrims should bear the shame longer. I hear the sound of the hammer, I see the smoke of the furnaces where manacles and fetters are still forged for human limbs.

"I pursue this topic no further, except again to say, that all Christendom, being now blessed with peace, is bound by everything which belongs to its character, and to the character of the present age, to put a stop to this inhuman and disgraceful traffic."

Finally Daniel addressed himself to the future generations who would enjoy what the people of New England were right then accomplishing. "We bid you welcome to this pleasant land of the fathers," he told them. "We welcome you to the blessings of good government and religious liberty. We welcome you to the immeasurable blessings of rational existence, the immortal hope of Christianity, and the light of everlasting truth."

Like George Ticknor, those who heard him speak that day were greatly moved, and the thousands of others who read the speech in print agreed that it was without a doubt the greatest speech ever yet given on the American continent.

Sacrifice and Sorrows

"Mr. Webster, I come to ask you to throw down your law books and enter the service of the public; for to the public you belong."

Daniel looked at the prominent men of Boston seated in his law office. They were his friends, men he knew well, the most influential men in the city. They were asking him to represent them in Congress, something he knew was a great honor. But he did not really want to accept. He had been in Congress before and did not feel his work was appreciated. He knew what the job paid, and it was not enough to support his family and pay for the debts he had inherited on the death of his father. Yet the men were very persuasive.

"I know what sacrifices we demand of you," they said, "but we must rely on your patriotism. We cannot take a refusal."

Webster knew they were right. He enjoyed his practice in Boston. He liked arguing cases before the Supreme Court and he was particularly fond of being

close to his family. Though he could continue to
practice before the Supreme Court in Washington,
he would have to sacrifice the income from his Boston
law practice and the time he enjoyed with his family.
Only the appeal to his patriotism was enough to compel those sacrifices.

"You can come to Washington again, as you did
before," he told Grace," "and we can write every
day."

Grace nodded sadly. She was proud of Daniel,
proud that the people of Boston thought he was the
best man to represent them in Washington, proud that
he was needed in the capitol to help run the affairs
of the country. Yet she was sad because once again
she and the children would have to share him with
the rest of the nation. It was not easy to learn about
his great speeches by reading them in the newspaper.
It was not easy to raise the children by herself. They
were in school now so there was no way the entire
family could live in Washington. She would have to
stay in Boston with the family once again.

The House of Representatives which Daniel entered
in December of 1823 was quite different from what
it had been when he left six years earlier. The
Federalist party had ceased to exist. The Democratic-
Republicans were the only party, but there were
various groups within that party which supported
many different men to succeed President Monroe
when his term was over. Each of these groups wanted
Webster to join them in support for their favorite candidate, but he decided to stay neutral as long he could.

One thing had not changed—Henry Clay was the
speaker of the House and he appointed Webster to
head the Judiciary Committee. In that position over
the next six years Webster demonstrated his ability
to write good legislation for the development and
growth of the nation.

Daniel kept his promise to write regularly to his family from Washington, and he corresponded with many other friends as well. Edward Everett, whom he had taught in Ezekiel's school in Boston, was now a writer for the "North American Review." He and Daniel had been writing each other about the battles for freedom then taking place in the country of Greece. A group of nations in Europe called the Holy Alliance were doing their best to see that democracy such as the United States enjoyed did not get a foothold in any European country. The Greeks struggling for independence had repeatedly appealed to America for help, and both Webster and Everett felt that we should at least recognize their struggle and send a representative to Greece to see first-hand what could be done.

"If nobody does it who can do it better," Daniel wrote to Everett, "I shall certainly say something of the Greeks. The miserable issue of the Spanish revolution makes the Greek cause more interesting, and I begin to think they have character enough to carry them through the contest with success."

For help in preparing his speech, he asked Everett to send him any information he had collected on the Greek campaigns. His friend was happy to help, and when Daniel rose to speak to the House of Representatives about the Greek question he had before him the many articles and papers Edward Everett had sent.

The speech was excellent. Everyone in Congress realized he was even more powerful in his oratory than before. But though they admired his oratory, they were not persuaded by his arguments. President Monroe had just spelled out his Monroe Doctrine in which he warned the nations of Europe, particularly the Holy Alliance, that they should not interfere with countries in the Western Hemisphere. Many of the men in Congress felt that if we did not want Europe to interfere on this continent, we should not interfere on the European continent. They thought that even sending a representative to Greece would be understood as interference, so Daniel's resolution did not pass. The speech, however, was translated into many foreign languages and made him famous not only in Greece but in many other countries as well. People were happy to know that there was a man in the United States willing to speak out for freedom in countries all over the world.

During December of that year Webster traveled with George Ticknor and his wife to visit in the homes of the former Presidents, James Madison and Thomas Jefferson. While at Monticello, Jefferson's home, a large snowstorm hit Virginia and they were snowed in for a week. The men enjoyed the opportunity to talk for hours with Jefferson about the great country they loved so well. The fact that they had once been political opponents was forgotten and Daniel wrote long letters to Grace about the visit with those great statesmen. It was almost like hearing his father once again telling stories of the Revolutionary War and the thrill of knowing George Washington, John Adams and Lafayette.

Upon returning to Washington after the snowstorm Daniel found a letter waiting from his wife. Their youngest child, Charlie, had become sick and died. Webster knew that there was nothing he could have done to save the boy if he had been in Boston, but it grieved his heart again to realize the sacrifice he was making, being constantly away from his family in order to serve his country.

Sitting down with a piece of paper, he wrote a poem to his son. It was the best way he knew to comfort his wife with the many miles between them.

> *"I held thee on my knee, my son!*
> *And kissed thee laughing, kissed thee weeping;*
> *But ah! thy little day is done,*
> *Thou art with thy angel sister sleeping.*
>
> *The staff on which my years should lean,*
> *Is broken, ere those years come o'er me;*
> *My funeral rites thou should'st have seen,*
> *But though art in the tomb before me.*
>
> *My father! I beheld thee born,*
> *And led thy tottering steps with care;*
> *Before me risen to Heaven's bright morn,*
> *My son! My Father! Guide me there."*

During the next session of Congress, Daniel spent most of his time rewriting the criminal codes of the United States. Justice Joseph Story of the Supreme Court was concerned that the criminal law had not been reviewed since the first Congress had sat. Counterfeiters were still being branded on the cheek while some states required the death penalty for anyone convicted of destroying a will. Story encouraged Daniel to codify the entire body of law, a huge job, and then introduce it in Congress as the "Crimes Act." This he did, supporting the act by his speeches and seeing the entire project approved by the Congress.

Then he went home to Boston for a much deserved vacation with his family. They were enjoying a Fourth of July celebration together in the town square, right in front of Independence Hall, when newsboys worked their way through the crowd with an extra edition of the paper.

"Extra, extra! Read all about it. Jefferson and Adams both dead. Extra, extra! Read all about it."

Quickly Daniel grabbed a paper and read as his family gathered around him. Thomas Jefferson and

John Adams had both died on the same day, the
fiftieth anniversary of the signing of the Declaration
of Independence. Both had been members of the Con-
tinental Congress and the committee to frame the
Declaration. Jefferson had written that document,
Adams had been its strongest defender. Each had
served as Vice-president and then as President of the
United States. Now they were both dead, on the
Fourth of July, exactly fifty years to the day since the
Declaration had been signed.

As Daniel read the story he thought of the week
in the snowstorm he had spent at Monticello. He
remembered the stories Jefferson told him about the
early years of the nation, and a speech began to form
itself in his mind. All he needed was a time and a place
to give it.

The oportunity came on August 2, 1826. The city
fathers of Boston held a commemoration service for
the two Presidents and invited Webster to give a public
discourse on their careers and service to the country.
The service was held in Faneuil Hall, a large
auditorium, but not large enough to hold the crowd
which gathered to hear Webster. When all the seats
were full the doors were pulled shut, leaving a great
crowd still outside. Webster saw it and stepped to the
edge of the platform. "Let the doors be opened," he
called. As his call was obeyed another crowd of people
made their way in to occupy every inch of standing
room. In spite of the crowded conditions, the people
stood quietly for more than two hours as Daniel
delivered his eulogy for Jefferson and Adams.

It was a strong speech, full of references to the great
work these two men had done in bringing America
to freedom. As Daniel told of the debate in the Con-
tinental Congress over the adoption of the Declaration of Independence, he told the audience the words

John Adams might have used in arguing for the Declaration.

"Sink or swim, live or die, survive or perish, I give my hand and my heart to this vote. It is true, indeed, that in the beginning we aimed not at independence. But there's a Divinity which shapes our ends. Is any man so weak as now to hope for a reconciliation with England, which shall leave either safety to the country and its liberties, or safety to his own life and his own honor? Do we mean to submit, and consent that we ourselves shall be ground to powder, and our country and its rights trodden down in the dust? I know we do not mean to submit. We never shall submit. All that I have, and all that I am, and all that I hope, in this life, I am now ready here to stake upon it; and I leave off as I began, that live or die, survive or perish, I am for the Declaration. It is my living sentiment, and by the blessing of God it shall be my dying sentiment, Independence now, and Independence for ever."

Many people thought that Daniel was quoting actual words from John Adams, but no records were kept of what was said in Congress. He told a friend later that he wrote the speech himself one morning after breakfast in his library as he thought Adams might have given it and "when it was finished my paper was wet with tears."

At the conclusion of his next term in the House friends in Boston encouraged him to run for the Senate. Webster consulted with friends in Washington, including President John Quincy Adams, who told him he was still needed in the House. So the Massachusetts state senate chose Levi Lincoln instead. But Lincoln did not accept the post. When the state senate met again they would not take no for an answer. Webster was elected to the United States Senate in 1827.

Grace had not been feeling well that spring, but recovered during the summer as the Websters and their children took an extended vacation on Cape Cod. She and the children enjoyed having Daniel to themselves, even though they knew it would not last long. When fall came and he had to return to Washington it was decided that Grace would go with him and the children would stay with friends in Boston for a time. Daniel was to join the Senate for the first time and Grace did not want to miss that important occasion in his life.

On their way to Washington they stopped in New York to visit friends. There Grace once again fell sick and the doctor announced that she had a tumor that was impossible for him to remove. Actually, she had tuberculosis. Even though she was very sick, Grace encouraged her husband to go on to Washington so as not to miss the opening of the Senate session. Finally he agreed after being assured by their friends and the doctor that she would have the finest of care and would soon recover and join him.

After two gloomy weeks in Washington the word from New York was still not good and Daniel made the trip back to be with his wife. For two more weeks she lingered, then one day asked that Daniel find a clergyman to come in and pray with her. She knew the end was near. Grace Webster died on January 21, 1828.

Daniel took the body back to Boston for burial and accompanied by the children followed the hearse on foot through the streets of the city to St. Paul's church where she was buried alongside Charlie. People there said it was the saddest funeral Boston had ever seen.

Although it was one of the most difficult things he had ever done, Daniel made himself return to Washington to continue his work in the Senate. He missed his wife tremendously, he loved her even more because they had been apart so much of the time.

Joseph Story, John Calhoun, Henry Clay and many others in Washington came to see Daniel and tell him how sorry they were about his loss. He appreciated their support, but he knew that the best way to recover was once again to get involved in his work.

Joseph Story wrote to George Ticknor that, "the very first day of Mr. Webster's arrival and taking his seat in the Senate there was a process bill on its third reading, filled, as he thought, with inconvenient and mischievous provisions." Daniel made some inquiries about the bill and "Mr. Tazewell from Virginia broke out upon him in a speech of two hours. Mr. Webster then moved an adjournment, and on the next day delivered a most masterly speech in reply."

In spite of his effort to recover by staying busy, Daniel found himself thinking often of Grace and how much he missed her. She had been a godly woman and had prayed often for him, and he missed her prayers. Many times she would write about her faith in the Lord and how she was providing for the spiritual training of the children. He realized how important that had been in his life as well as the lives of Daniel Fletcher, Julia and Edward.

The one who understood his sorrow the best was his brother Ezekiel. Ezekiel had also lost his wife after years of marriage and even though he was now remarried he remembered the tremendous sense of loneliness which had possessed him. Both he and his wife wrote long letters to Daniel, trying to encourage him to keep going in his work in Washington.

"I am growing indolent," Daniel wrote back. "I do nothing in Congress but what is clearly necessary."

Ezekiel invited Daniel to visit that summer and they had a good time together planning Zeke's campaign for the House of Representatives in the spring election of 1829. Daniel looked forward to having his brother with him in Washington. But Ezekiel, even though he was a good lawyer, did not have his brother's ability to move the hearts of the people. He was defeated in his bid for election.

That March, Andrew Jackson was inaugurated as President of the United States. Following the celebration in Washington, Daniel traveled to Boston to visit his children. There he was to meet Ezekiel's wife and daughter and the two families were going to travel to Salisbury to spend a few days on the old farm place. Daniel was planning to show the children places which were so dear to him from his childhood.

Early on the morning they were to leave Boston a young man came knocking on the door. "I have a message from Concord, New Hampshire, for Senator Daniel Webster," he called.

As Daniel went down to answer the door he knew it had to be something concerning his brother, but he had no idea how serious it was.

"Senator Webster?" The boy shifted back and forth from foot to foot. "Your brother, Ezekiel? He was speaking to a jury at the Court House in Concord yesterday, and he dropped dead, right there in front of them."

"Oh, no," gasped Daniel. "Not Ezekiel. Not my brother, too."

We the People...

12

State's Rights Versus Union

The death of his brother Ezekiel was almost as great a loss as the death of his wife. Ezekiel had helped him through school, had arranged for him to get his start in Boston, had supported him politically in New Hampshire and had faithfully written to encourage him in his stand for the Constitution. Daniel greatly missed his support and friendship.

Many encouraged Webster to remarry, feeling that he needed a wife to share the burden of his work as well as to hostess the social functions at which he was expected to entertain important guests. Although he still missed Grace very much, Daniel began to watch for someone who could take her place in his life.

On December 12, 1829, he married Caroline LeRoy, the daughter of a New York businessman who had been one of his clients in various court cases. Caroline went with him to Washington where they settled into a boardingroom in a doctor's residence.

Daniel wanted to give his new bride the best of everything, so he bought a carriage and hired a maid and a footman. Soon all the important people in Washington came to call on the new Mrs. Webster, and she worried about how to pronounce the foreign names and how to repay all the invitations they received to other people's houses. She was very happy to be the wife of the famous Senator Webster.

Within a month of the wedding the new session of Congress began. Although the previous twenty years had been known as the "Era of Good Feelings" in Washington, those feelings were beginning to change. In the summer of 1828 John C. Calhoun, vice president of the United States and a former Congressman from South Carolina, wrote *The South Carolina Exposition and Protest*. Many Southerners were upset about laws being passed by Congress which they thought were written only to hurt the Southern states.

In his paper Calhoun agreed that since the states had originally ratified the Constitution through state conventions, each state still had the right to decide which laws of the United States they wanted to obey and which ones they did not want to obey. This idea became known as "nullification" because South Carolina in particular wanted to "nullify" a law known as the Tariff of 1828. Calhoun believed that each state, acting through state conventions, could refuse to keep national laws they thought were unconstitutional.

Webster read Calhoun's paper while he was still mourning the death of his wife. He talked about it with Ezekiel just before he died. He remembered how his father and his brother had loved their country, how Ebenezer had fought to defend it against England, and how Ezekiel had written so many times to encourage him in his stand for the Constitution.

He thought of his first Fourth of July speech to the people of Hanover, and how he had praised President George Washington and the Constitution. He remembered his Plymouth oration, his Dartmouth College case before the Supreme Court and his eulogy for Adams and Jefferson. In each of them he had described in glowing terms the glorious liberty accomplished through that great document which Jefferson and others had produced. It made him sad that John Calhoun, who was a friend and had once defended the nation just as strongly as Webster, was now advocating the rights of the states over the unity of the nation. Support of the Constitution and a united nation had always been important to Daniel, but now when it was faced with this challenge he thought about it more than ever.

Opportunity to speak about his views on the Constitution came in an unusual way. About three weeks into the session which started after his wedding, Senator Foote from Massachusetts offered a simple resolution to consider limiting the sale of public lands. Senator Thomas Hart Benton of Missouri charged that the resolution was an attempt by the eastern states to stop further settlement in the west.

The matter would perhaps have been dropped there, but the next day Senator Robert Y. Hayne of South Carolina decided to give a speech in support of Senator Benton. Although John Calhoun had just been elected vice president under Andrew Jackson, Hayne was already looking ahead to the next election. He wanted Calhoun to be President of the United States, and he knew that in order for that to happen there would have to be an alliance between the western and southern states. If he could get Senator Benton on Calhoun's side, perhaps other men from the west would help the south as well.

In Senator Hayne's speech he drew a word picture
of the poor conditions on the western frontier. He
described how settlers were robbed of their money by
the federal govenment which then turned around and
spent the money, not to improve roads in the west,
but to benefit the already rich eastern states. He called
the United States a "stepmother" who was charging
the poor western settlers for land which they should
have been giving away. He said it was the intention
of Senator Foote and others from the eastern states
to keep the western settlers in poverty so that the "rich
proprietors of the woolen and cotton factories" could
get richer. That was a direct attack on New England
since that is where the cotton and woolen factories
were located.

Daniel did not hear the first speech of Senator Ben-
ton, but he returned from an appearance before the
Supreme Court just in time to hear the end of
Senator's Hayne's speech.

The next day he rose to reply to the charges of the
senator from South Carolina. He explained how
ridiculous it was to think that the eastern states were
trying to keep the west from developing. "The government has been no stepmother to the new states," he
said. "She has not been careless of their interests, nor
deaf to their requests. From the very origin of the
government these western lands and the just protection of the settlers have been the leading object of our
policy. The Indian titles have been extinguished at
the expense of many millions. Is that nothing?" In
every instance Hayne had cited, Daniel showed that
the goverment had helped the West rather than
hurting it.

But Webster did not stop there. He knew what was
behind Hayne's attack on the East and he felt that
it had gone far enough. "I rise to defend the East,"
he continued, "I rise to repel both the charge itself

and the cause assigned for it. I deny that the East has at any time shown an ill-liberal policy toward the West. I pronounce the whole accusation to be without the least foundation.''

With his strongest lion-like emotions aroused, he questioned Hayne's loyalty to the Union itself. He accused the senator of believing that ''the Union is to be preserved while it suits local and temporary purposes to preserve it; and to be sundered whenever it shall be found to thwart such purposes.'' That was exactly what Hayne did believe. He supported Calhoun's doctrine of nullification, believing that the laws of the Union could be overthrown by decisions of the individual states. Sitting and listening to the entire discussion, as head of the Senate, was the author of the nullification doctrine, Vice President John C. Calhoun.

Now Senator Hayne was angry, and he let it be known that on the next day he would reply to Senator Webster and tell him just exactly what he thought of not only his state but Daniel himself. When Webster arrived in the Senate chambers the next day he could hardly make his way through the lobby it was so crowded. Every seat in the Senate gallery was filled and many senators were standing around the walls, having given up their seats on the floor to the southern belles who had come to hear Robert Hayne champion the cause of the South.

Before either Benton or Hayne could begin speaking, a friend of Daniel's asked that further discussion of the resolution be postponed until Monday since Webster had another appointment outside of the Senate that day but did not want to miss the discussion.

Hayne had his crowd on hand and he objected. ''I see the gentleman from Massachusetts in his seat, and

presume he could make an arrangement which would
enable him to be present. The gentleman has
discharged his fire in the face of the Senate,'' Hayne
said. ''I hope he will now afford me the opportunity
of returning the shot.''

Daniel rose from his seat and nodded toward the
senator. ''I am ready to receive it. Let the discussion
proceed.''

Both Benton and Hayne spoke that day, and
Hayne's speech carried over until Monday when the
Senate chambers were even more crowded than
before. On this occasion Hayne made a bitter attack
on New England, railed upon Mr. Webster personally
as he had said he would do and then launched into
a defense of slavery as if it were a blessing. He
described the Union as a weak organization made up
of strong independent states. It was not proper
according to him to use tax money raised in South
Carolina to build roads or railroads in other states.
During the course of the speech messengers were seen
carrying notes to him from Calhoun, who was
presiding over the Senate. Hayne used them to give
a long detailed defense of the Calhoun doctrine of
nullification. The speech lasted until late in the day,
giving Webster time only to ask for permission to
bring his reply on the following day.

Supporters of Hayne went home that night confident that there was no way Daniel Webster or anyone
else could answer the speech that their champion had
given.

At the same time supporters of Webster encouraged
each other, some confidently, some hopefully. News
of the debate had spread throughout the country and
many from New York and even further north rode
down to find out what was being said. The greatest
crowd ever to assemble in the Senate building packed

the chamber and the lobby and the halls the next day. Some southerners stayed away, thinking it was all over, but their places were taken by the many who had come in from New England.

As the Senate was called to order that morning and the chaplain led in prayer a hush fell over the crowd. Slowly Daniel Webster rose to his feet. Sleepily he turned toward Calhoun, the president of the senate and began to speak in a quiet, conversational tone of voice.

"Mr. President," he began. "When the mariner has been tossed for many days in the thick weather, and on an unknown sea, he naturally avails himself of the first pause in the storm, the earliest glance of the sun, to take his latitude, and ascertain how far the elements have driven him from his true course. Let us imitate this prudence, and before we float further on the waves of this debate, refer to the point from which we departed, that we may at least be able to conjecture where we now are. I ask for the reading of the resolution before the Senate."

Those who had expected him to launch into an immediate attack on Hayne were surprised, but not the ones who knew Daniel best. He was recalling how his friend Jeremiah Mason had talked quietly to the juries in New Hampshire in words they could understand and he was preparing to do the same. Far more than Hayne, Webster realized that he was not just speaking to the people in the Senate chamber. He was defending the nation and the Constitution before every man and woman in the United States. Attacking Robert Hayne might satisfy those who were listening that day, but there was a more important job to do, one which God had been preparing him for all his life. He had the job of preserving the Union.

After the resolution was read, Daniel started

talking again. "We have thus heard, Sir, what the resolution is which is actually before us for consideration; and it will readily occur to everyone, that it is almost the only subject about which something has not been said in the speech, running through two days, by which the Senate has been entertained by the gentleman from South Carolina." Many people laughed when Daniel said that because they knew it was true. Hayne had covered many topics but had said nothing about the original resolution. "To that subject, in all his excursions, he had not paid even the cold respect of a passing glance," Daniel went on.

"He had a shot, he said, to return," Webster referred to Hayne's insistence that he stay for the speech the previous week, "and he wished to discharge it. That shot has now been received. If nobody is found after all either killed or wounded it is not the first time, in the history of human affairs, that the vigor and success of the war have not quite come up to the lofty and sounding phrase of the manifesto." Again the audience laughed while Mr. Hayne stared angrily at the speaker. Already Daniel had most of the crowd on his side.

"The gentleman, Sir, in declining to postpone the debate, told the Senate, with the emphasis of his hand upon his heart, that there was something rankling here which he wished to relieve."

Although Webster had sat quietly through two days of Hayne's speech, the South Carolina senator was so angry that he could not stay silent as Webster had. He jumped to his feet, interrupting the speech. "I did not use the word rankling," he yelled.

Undisturbed, Daniel went on, "It would not, Mr. President, be safe for the honorable member to appeal to those around him, upon the question whether he did in fact make use of that word. But he may have been unconscious of it."

After a few more words of introduction in which he made light of Senator Hayne's personal attacks upon him, Webster set about to answer the real issues in the debate. He defended the right of the government to sell public lands and showed how that money had been used to improve the West, with New England strongly supporting the improvements. He gave many illustrations of specific incidents where he and other men from the East had supported measures favoring the West. Item by item, without ever referring to the twelve pages of notes he had brought with him, he answered the issues which Hayne had raised, moving all the time closer to what he felt was the main issue—nullification.

He approached the main issue by taking exception to Hayne's remarks about using South Carolina tax money to help other states. "Here we differ," he said. "I look upon a road over the Alleghanies, a canal round the falls of the Ohio, or a canal or railway from the Atlantic to the western waters, as being an object large and extensive enough to be fairly said to be for the common benefit." Everyone knew this was true because only a few days earlier Webster had presented a petition from the South Carolina Canal and Railroad company asking the federal government to subscribe to its capital stock on grounds that its projected railroad would aid the national welfare.

"The states are One," Webster thundered, talking clearly and rapidly now like the roused lion he became when he was full of his topic and ready to unload. "In war and peace we are one; in commerce, one; because the authority of the general government reaches to war and peace, and to the regulation of commerce."

Daniel was now prepared to advance his main argument, that the Constitution did not come from the agreement of individual states, but from the people within those states. It was the creation not of independent states, but of a people who chose that means of binding themselves together into one great nation. "The Constitution of the United States is the people's Constitution," he told the crowd. "It is made for the people, by the people and is answerable to the people. The people of the United States have declared this Constitution shall be the supreme law of the land. It is created for one purpose, the state governments for another. To make war, for instance, is an exercise of sovereignty, but the Constitution declares that no state shall make war. Again the Constitution says that no state shall be so sovereign as to make a treaty."

Now Daniel was talking about that which was dearest to his heart, and the people listening could tell how much it meant to him. It was almost as if the words were thunderbolts which were dropping to him out of the sky while he grabbed them and flung them back at the listening crowd.

"I profess, Sir, in my career hitherto, to have kept steadily in view the prosperity and honor of the whole country, and the preservation of our Federal Union. It is to that Union we owe our safety at home, and our consideration and dignity abroad. It is to that Union that we are chiefly indebted for whatever makes us most proud of our country. Every year of its duration has teemed with fresh proofs of its utility and its blessings; and although our territory has stretched out wide and wider, and our population spread further and further, they have not outrun its protection nor its benefits."

Although many had been standing for hours, there was not a sound heard through the Senate chambers except the sound of Mr. Webster's voice as he brought his great speech to a conclusion.

"When my eyes shall be turned to behold for the last time the sun in heaven, may I not see him shining on the broken and dishonored fragments of a once glorious Union; on States dissevered, discordant, belligerent; on a land rent with civil feuds, or drenched, it may be, in fraternal blood. Let their last feeble and lingering glance rather behold the gorgeous ensign of the republic, now known and honored throughout the earth, still full high advanced, its arms and trophies streaming in their original lustre, not a stripe erased or polluted, nor a single star obscured, bearing for its motto no such miserable interrogatory as 'What is all this worth?' nor those other words of delusion and folly, 'Liberty first and Union afterwards,' but everywhere, spread all over in characters of living light, blazing on all its ample folds, as they float over the sea and over the land, and in every wind under the whole heavens, that other sentiment, dear to every true Ameican heart—Liberty and Union, now and for ever, one and inseparable!''

The people cheered, and some were in tears. Many who heard the speech or who read it later, had not realized the importance of the Union and the Constitution in their own lives. Webster's oldest son, Daniel Fletcher, wrote to his father after reading the speech that, "I never knew what the Constitution really was, till your last short speech. I thought it was a compact between the states."

Not everyone, of course, agreed with Webster. That evening at a White House party, Daniel found himself standing next to Senator Hayne.

"How are you this evening?" he asked graciously.

"None the better for you," Hayne barked.

Later President Jackson rose to offer a toast, and moved by Daniel's speech himself, used the words which had stirred all the listeners. "Our Federal Union: it must be preserved," said the President.

Then it was Vice President Calhoun's turn to propose a toast. Glaring over at Webster he spoke out bitterly, "Our Federal Union: next to our liberties, the most dear."

A deep hush settled over the room, but Daniel turned away sadly without replying and the party broke up because people were so embarrassed at Calhoun's lack of courtesy.

In spite of those who criticized there was no doubt, however, that Washington had just witnessed the delivery of the greatest speech America had ever heard.

We the People...

13

The Issue of Nullification

"Daniel, have you seen it?" Caroline Webster rushed into the study of their Washington apartment where her husband was reading. "Someone has published a collection of your speeches. They've put them in a book so everyone can read them."

Webster took the leather-bound book from his wife and opened the cover. The reply to Hayne had been published in almost every newspaper in the country as had many of his other speeches. Now a publisher had taken several of those previously published speeches and put them together into a book. Inside the front cover was a sketch of his likeness done by an artist he had never heard of. Daniel stared at the picture for a time, and then leafed through the rest of the book.

"Well enough," he said, handing it back to his wife, "except for the awful face. They must have placed that in the front of the volume, like a scarecrow in a cornfield, to frighten off all intruders."

In spite of his comment, Webster was pleased that

people were interested enough in his speeches to purchase them. He received letters from all over the United States and from many foreign countries praising him for the reply to Hayne. "I return my thanks," President Madison wrote, "for the copy of your late very powerful speech in the Senate of the United States. It crushes nullification and must hasten an abandonment of secession." His old friend and sometime political opponent Henry Clay wrote, "I congratulate you on the very great addition which you have made during the present session to your previous high reputation. Your speeches, and particularly that in reply to Mr. Hayne, are the theme of praise from every tongue; and I have shared in the delight which all have felt. I trust that they will do much good."

Henry Clay was at that time in a private practice of law in Kentucky, but many, including Daniel, were encouraging him to run for president against Andrew Jackson in 1832. Friends from Massachusetts wanted Daniel to run, and he would have been willing to do so, but he felt that Clay was the better candidate at that time. There was still only one political party, but those who wanted Jackson to serve a second term were called Democratic-Republicans and those who wanted Henry Clay to be president were call National-Republicans. Most of the old Federalists like Webster were part of the National-Republicans.

The National-Republicans met in convention at Baltimore on December 12, 1831, and nominated Clay unanimously for President. After the convention adjourned, Webster and a Massachusetts congressman, Nathan Appleton, hosted a dinner for the new presidential nominee.

With the election coming up the new session of Congress became one of great importance. Supporters of President Jackson wanted to get rid of the Bank of the United States by refusing to renew its charter while those opposed to Jackson wanted to see the charter extended. Webster defended the bank in the Senate and a new charter was passed by both houses of Congress.

President Jackson decided to veto the new charter. In doing so he put forth an unusual new argument. He said that although the Supreme Court had decided a national bank was constitutional, he had the right as chief executive to regard the bank unconstitutional. "The Congress, the Executive and the Court," he said, "must each for itself be guided by its own opinion of the Constitution. Each public officer who takes a public oath to support the Constitution swears that he will support it as he understands it, and not as it is understood by others. The opinion of the judges has no more authority over Congress than the opinion of Congress has over the judges; and on that point, the President is independent of both.'' In effect he was advocating his own doctrine of nullification but this time it was not the states that could ignore a law, it was the President who could personally choose which laws to obey and which not to obey.

The next day it was Daniel's job to answer this strange argument in the Senate as they prepared to vote a second time on the measure. In his calm and unhurried fashion he showed how the acceptance of such a doctrine would completely destroy the Supreme Court, taking away the balance of power the framers of the Constitution had been so careful to maintain. ''When a law has been passed by Congress and approved by the President, it is now no longer in the power, either of the same president, or of his successors, to say whether the law is constitutional or not. He is not at liberty to disregard it; and to nullify it if he so chooses. In the courts that question may be raised, argued and adjudged nowhere else.''

''It is the law now existing, passed by Congress, approved by President Madison, and sanctioned by a solemn judgment of the Supreme Court, which he now declares unconstitutional. If these opinions of the President be maintained, there is an end of all law and all judicial authority. Statutes are but recommendations, judgments no more than opinions.''

It was another great speech and although there were not enough votes to overturn the veto and the bank charter was not renewed, the opinion that a president has the right to declare a law unconstitutional in opposition to the Court was never suggested again by Jackson or any other president.

The fight over the bank divided the followers of

Jackson and those who opposed him even more. They were more determined than ever to see Henry Clay elected president. Instead, Jackson was reelected by a large marjority.

Soon after the election an issue arose which brought Webster to the support of President Jackson. Congress voted to renew a tariff bill which South Carolina did not like, and that state held a convention and adopted an ordinance declaring the bill "null, void, and no law."

Although John C. Calhoun and Robert Hayne had talked about nullification, no state had ever before actually tried it. Many people, including Webster, believed that President Jackson would be slow to respond to such a crisis. They thought that he might even secretly approve of nullification, but they were surprised. Almost immediately he issued a proclamation to the people of South Carolina specifically denying their right to nullify a law. "I consider the power to annul a law of the United States, assumed by one state, incompatible with the existence of the Union, contradicted expressly by the letter of the Constitution, unauthorized by its spirit, inconsistent with every principle on which it was founded, and destructive of the great object for which it was formed," read the proclamation. It was just as strong as any statement Webster had ever made.

Calhoun, having resigned as vice president was once again back in the Senate, replacing Hayne who had been elected governor of South Carolina. He was defending the right of his state to nullification at every opportunity.

Early in 1833 President Jackson asked Congress to pass a bill which would make it possible for him to meet the resistance of South Carolina to the Union. Calhoun immediately labeled this the "Force Bill."

Since many of Jackson's supporters were southerners and had no intention of speaking against South Carolina, members of the administration appealed to Webster to support the bill. The debate continued for several weeks until Senator Calhoun, on February 15 and 16, delivered a long speech against the "Force Bill" and in favor of nullification. Many who heard it said it was much better than Hayne's speech in defense of nullification, but Daniel's remark was, "I was greatly disappointed in Mr. Calhoun. He has little argument—at least so it appeared to me."

Even though he was disappointed in the speech, it was necessary for him to answer it, and that put him in support of the Jackson administration. Then, as throughout all his life, the principles of the Union were greater to him than party loyalties. That was what made him the great statesman he was. On the day he was to reply, the President's personal carriage pulled up to their door, to the surprise of Caroline. Daniel received a message of support from Jackson and then the carriage took him and Caroline to the Senate where the speech would be given.

John Calhoun's two days of speaking had been marked by bitter attacks on many people and threats against the administration and the Union itself. As Daniel rose to speak he began quietly, but firmly, to state once again his position on the Union.

"The gentleman has terminated his speech in a tone of threat and defiance towards this bill, even should it become a law of the land, altogether unusual in the halls of Congress. But I shall not suffer myself to be excited into warmth by his denunciation of the measure which I support."

True to his word, Webster proceeded to give reasonable strong arguments in support for what he believed, rather than engaging in bitter name-calling. In some ways he covered the same ground as in his reply to Hayne, but he answered in detail Calhoun's belief that the Constitution was simply a compact between sovereign states.

"I maintain that the Constitution of the United States is not a league, confederacy, or compact between the people of the several states in their sovereign capacities; but a government proper, founded on the adoption of the people, and creating direct relations between itself and individuals," he stated. Then, after proving that from the Constitution itself, he warned that the doctrine of nullification was in fact a doctrine of revolution. He stated that if the doctrine of nullification was followed it would undoubtedly lead to war. But he was not threatening war, as Calhoun had; instead, he was trying to bring men to a place of reason. He still had great hope for the Union. "Depend upon it, sir," he concluded. "If we can avoid the shock of arms, a day for reconsideration and reflection will come; truth and reason will act with their accustomed force, and the public opinion of South Carolina will be restored to its usual constitutional and patriotic tone."

No other speech of Daniel's had been so close and powerful in its reasoning, and if it did not arouse the same response as the earlier reply to Hayne, it was because it covered much of the same material. The "Force Bill" was passed overwhelmingly by both houses of Congress. At the same time they passed a compromise tariff bill proposed by Henry Clay that lowered the tariff to which the people of South Carolina were objecting. Cautiously the nation moved back from the threat of civil war, and Daniel's Union was preserved.

The Slavery Problem

During the debate between Webster and Calhoun over the Force Bill it became obvious to many people that the southern states were willing, if necessary, to secede from the Union to protect what they considered to be their rights, including slavery. These people, especially those in Massachusetts, realized that it would take strong leadership in Washington to preserve the Union. They could think of no one better to provide that leadership than the defender of the Constitution, Daniel Webster. Once again they began to campaign to nominate him for president.

President Jackson was known to favor Martin Van Buren to be his successor. Those opposed to Jackson's policy on the bank and those opposed to his policy on nullification became known as the Whigs. Their obvious leader was Henry Clay who appealed to the southerners because he was from Kentucky and to the old National Republicans because he was against Jackson. But Clay had been nominated in 1832 and had lost so there were many who wanted to give

Webster a chance. Rather than wait for a party convention, Jeremiah Mason, Edward Everett and others in Massachusetts met in a state convention and nominated Daniel as their candidate for president of the United States. They hoped that the Whig Party would follow their action and nominate him as well. It was Daniel's desire to lead a party which would be known for its allegiance to the Union and support for the Constitution.

When the Whig Party met in December of 1835 Daniel's friends were confident he would be chosen. However, there were many groups within the Whig Party who wanted him to promise that if he were elected he would turn Jackson's political appointments out of office and give the jobs to them. Webster replied that it was not consistent with his sense of duty "to hold out promises, or anything that might be regarded as equivalent to promises, particularly on the eve of a great election, the results of which are to affect the highest interests of the country for years to come."

Henry Clay, who was at the convention, would not support Daniel either, and when President Jackson heard that, he predicted, "Mr. Webster won't be nominated because he is too far East, knows too much and is too honest."

Jackson was right. Upset with Webster for not promising them jobs, some groups gave their support to General William Henry Harrison, the great military hero of the War of 1812. Others in favor of nullification chose candidates who would support that position. So the Whig Party broke into factions, and in the election Martin Van Buren was chosen as the next President.

Disappointed with the results of the election and deeply in debt because of the small salary which Congressmen were paid, Daniel decided to resign from

public life and return to Boston to be a lawyer. He
was also in debt because of Jackson's policies with the
United States Bank. President Van Buren continued
to fight the bank, and in 1837 the country had a financial depression. Thousands of businessmen and banks
were ruined. It looked for a time as if the Websters
would lose Marshfield, their beautiful home in Boston.

When his friends learned of Daniel's intention they
were horrified. "The Union needs you in
Washington," they pleaded with him. "If it were not
for you the policies of the administration would have
put American merchants and industrialists totally at
the mercy of the government. You have all your life
long fought the battle for us. You can't leave now."

In order to help persuade him, and help pay his debts, Edward Everett went to many of Daniel's friends in Massachusetts and New York and appealed to them to put together a substantial gift of money in honor of his great leadership. They also planned a reception in his honor which was held at Niblo's Garden in New York City on March 15, 1837.

Invited to address the large crowd of friends who gathered to honor him that evening, Daniel announced that their persuasion had worked. "Those whose opinions I am bound to respect saw objections to a present withdrawal from Congress; I have yielded my own strong desire to their convictions of what the public good desires."

Then he went on to outline where the country stood at that time and where he wanted to see it go. One of the biggest issues facing the nation at that time involved Texas. Having won their independence from Mexico they had set up their own government and were now applying for admission to the Union. Webster opposed this for one reason. "Texas is likely to be a slave-holding country; and I frankly avow my entire unwillingness to do anything that shall extend the slavery of the African race on this continent, or add other slave-holding states to the Union."

Daniel had expressed his views on slavery before, and it was becoming obvious to him and others that this was really the issue at the heart of the nullification doctrine and he wanted everyone to know exactly where he stood. "Slavery, as it exists in the states is beyond the reach of Congress. It is a concern of the states themselves; they have never submitted it to Congress, and Congress has no rightful power over it. But when we come to speak of admitting new states, the subject assumes an entirely different aspect. On the general question of slavery, a great portion of the community is already strongly excited. It has arrested the religious feeling of the country; it has taken strong hold on the consciences of men.''

Webster's own conscience was disturbed by slavery as well. Though it was legal to own slaves in some states and he believed in obeying the law, he was willing to leave those states alone. But he was not willing to allow them to extend slavery to other states as well. On that basis he opposed the admittance of Texas as a state.

Once again this speech was published and read throughout the nation. Daniel began to get requests from many places to visit and share with them his views on the Union and the Constitution. So in the summer of 1837 he and Caroline, along with their daughter Julie and another couple, made a trip through the West. Public dinners were held in his honor at Lexington, Louisville, Cincinnati and St. Louis, each one including a speech. From there he went on to Chicago and then back through Detroit, Toledo and Buffalo, New York. One result of this trip was to again push him into the front as a presidential candidate for the next election. It was becoming

obvious that the financial policies of President Van
Buren were not working and it looked as if the Whigs
would have an easy time defeating him in 1840.

As much as he wanted to be president, there were
other matters which were even more important. He
believed that God had given him his position in
Washington so that he could work to preserve the
Union, and the issue which was more and more
dividing that Union was slavery.

.John Calhoun was not satisfied with Webster's
speech at the Niblo Gardens. He did not believe that
the East would be content to leave the slave states alone
if Texas was not admitted to the Union. In fact, others
in the North, unlike Webster, worked actively to
abolish slavery, particularly in the District of
Columbia where the city of Washington sat.

In order to protect slavery in the District of Columbia, Calhoun offered a resolution which said in part
that, "the intermeddling of any state or states, or their
citizens, to abolish slavery in this District, or any of
the Territories, on the ground, or under the pretext,
that it is immoral or sinful, or the passage of any act
or measure of Congress with that view, would be a
direct and dangerous attack on the institution of all
the slave-holding states."

Such language was directly opposed to the view
Webster expressed earlier that year at Niblo's Garden.
There he made it clear that although slavery was still
legal, he found it both immoral and sinful, against
his religious convictions and his conscience. Calhoun's
resolution, then, was designed with him in mind, as
well as those who were actually pressing for the aboli-
tion of slavery.

Two weeks later Henry Clay offered a substitute
for Calhoun's resolution in which he stated that since
Maryland and Virginia had given the land for the

District of Columbia to the United States, it would
be a violation of their rights as states to pass a law
abolishing slavery in the District. Such an act, Mr.
Clay stated would "disturb and endanger the Union."

What Calhoun and Clay were actually saying was
that Congress did not have the right to abolish slavery
in the District because that would violate the states'
rights of Maryland and Virginia. Here was nullification in still another form.

Immediately Daniel rose to his feet to speak against
the Clay and Calhoun resolution. "The words of the
Constitution are clear and plain," he said. "Congress,
by that instrument, has power to exercise exclusive
jurisdiction over the ceded territory, in all cases what-
soever."

Then to the great embarrassment of the senators
from Kentucky and South Carolina he quoted from
the very deed Virginia and Maryland had given to
the United States, showing that the government had
been given "full and absolute right and exclusive
jurisdiction, as well of soil as of persons residing or
to reside therein." Once again his tremendous
memory provided him the materials he needed to support his case. He did not go on and state at that time
his opinion on whether slavery should be abolished
in the District, but he completely destroyed the argument that the government did not have the right to
abolish it if they so chose.

Because it had been necessary to oppose not only
Calhoun, but also Clay, in the Senate, Daniel realized
that the Whig Party would not be able to turn to either
him or Henry Clay and expect to display any kind
of unity. So in the summer of 1839 he and Caroline
planned a trip to Europe. Before they left he let it be
known that he was not to be nominated for president
for the election of 1840.

The Websters, accompanied again by Julia, arrived in London on June 5th and took lodging at the Brunswick Hotel. The next morning Mrs. Webster looked out the window to find the street lined with expensive carriages.

"There must be a great meeting of some kind being held here at the hotel," she told her husband. "Look at all the carriages."

"Amazing," Daniel said as he joined her at the window. "I have not been informed of any such event."

But it was not a meeting at all. Instead, the leading citizens of London had gathered for a glimpse of the man whose fame in oratory had spread even across the ocean. For the next two months they offered him their hospitality. The Websters were entertained by William Wordsworth, Thomas Carlyle, Charles Dickens and many more. England had already abolished slavery under the strong leadership of William Wilberforce and they were watching with interest what was taking place in their former colonies. They had heard about the man who more than any other was working to preserve the Union, and they wanted to see him and hear him for themselves.

The impression Webster made on the people of England was great. "No man can be so wise as Webster looks," said Sydney Smith. Thomas Carlyle called him, "a magnificent specimen, as a logic-fencer, advocate, or parliamentary Hercules, one would incline to back him at first sight against all the extant world."

Mrs. Webster and Julia kept diaries and recorded all the sights they saw in England and on the continent. Daniel's favorite activity was to take a carriage over to Parliament and listen to the great orators of England as they debated. He was far more interested in the ideas of men and the way they expressed them than he was in sightseeing.

Upon their return to the states he was greeted with news that William Henry Harrison had again been nominated for president by the Whigs. The states' rights advocates had tried to balance the ticket with a senator from Virginia named John Tyler. Because of General Harrison's victory over the Indians at Tippecanoe they were running under the slogan, "Tippecanoe and Tyler too." Confident of a Whig victory over President Van Buren, Daniel began traveling the country speaking in support of "Tippecanoe." The time had finally come to unite the country under the Whig Party.

Webster as Secretary of State

The election of 1840 was one of the noisiest in history. The Whigs did not agree on a party platform, so they just attacked the record of President Van Buren who was running for reelection as a Democrat. In turn, Democratic newspapers looked for something about General William Harrison which they could attack. They didn't want to say anything bad about his war record; that would have been unpatriotic. Finally a newspaper in Baltimore made the remark that Harrison was more suited for life in a log cabin with a barrel of hard cider by his side than he was for the White House. Instead of turning people against the Whig candidate by that comment, the paper actually succeeded in giving the Whigs an argument in favor of their candidate.

Daniel Webster read the article in the Baltimore paper and accused the Democrats of sneering ''at whatever savors of humble life.'' William Harrison became known as the "Log Cabin" candidate and all over the country "Tippecanoe clubs" held log cabin raisings, sported log cabin badges and sang log cabin songs. Magazines and song books with pictures of Harrison sitting on the porch of a log cabin were seen everywhere.

Since General Harrison had never been a public figure and was not a good speaker, the man everyone wanted to hear during the course of the election was Daniel Webster. He accepted invitations from all across the states and gave great speeches in Saratoga, New York and Richmond. At a Bunker Hill celebration in Boston an estimated seventy-five thousand people heard him at one time. Each audience was thrilled to hear the great orator speak.

"It did not happen to me to be born in a log cabin," he told them. "But my elder brothers and sisters were born in a log cabin, raised amid the snowdrifts of New Hampshire at a period so early that when the smoke first rose from its rude chimney and curled over the frozen hills there was no similar evidence of a white man's habitation between it and the settlements on the rivers of Canada. Its remains still exist. I make an annual visit to it. I carry my children to it, to teach them of the hardships endured by generations which have gone before them."

General Harrison won the election. Whigs were for the first time in control of the national govenrment. The new President invited Daniel to become a part of his cabinet as Secretary of State, so he resigned from his Senate seat to accept the new job. One of his first tasks was to help Harrison write his inaugural address.

General Harrison had written a flowery speech full of references to Roman history. Daniel persuaded him to leave out most of those references. When he returned home that night Caroline met him at the door.

"Daniel, what has happened? You look positively exhausted tonight."

"You would think that something happened if you know what I have done," he said. "I have killed seventeen Roman proconsuls today."

The day of the inauguration was a chilly one in Washington. The speech went well and then it was time for the parade. The great soldier, Harrison, insisted on riding his horse in the parade. His dress clothes in which he gave the speech were not much protection against the weather, however, and that night he came down with a bad cold. The cold developed into pneumonia and a month later, on March 4, he died.

No president had ever before died in office, and even though the Constitution called for the vice president to take over in case of the president's death there were some who didn't think John Tyler was legally entitled to become the chief executive. Webster had no doubt that such was the intent of the Constitution, but no one knew for sure where the Vice President was.

As the senior member in the cabinet, Daniel decided he was the one to do something, so he sent his oldest son Daniel Fletcher to look for Tyler.

The Vice President wasn't anywhere in Washington. Fletcher had to ride all the way to Williamsburg, Virginia, to find Tyler on the plantation where he lived. When he got there Tyler was down on his hands and knees playing marbles.

"Excuse me, Mr. Tyler. I have a message from my father, Daniel Webster. He says that it would be best for you to come back to Washington right away, sir. You are now the President of the United States."

Even though John Tyler was now the President there were many people who did not like him. One of these was Henry Clay. He was still the leader of the Whig Party and he did not think Tyler was a good Whig. Tyler had been placed on the ticket to try to attract Democrat votes. No one really thought he would become the president.

Clay contacted each member of the cabinet, all of whom were Whigs, and told them to resign. Five did, but not Daniel. Even though he did not agree with President Tyler on everything, Tyler was now the president and Daniel believed that he needed his support.

For a number of years there had been a dispute between Canada and the states of Maine and Vermont concerning the border between them. More than once battles broke out in that area, and war was a constant danger. When Daniel became Secretary of State he wanted to settle that disagreement, so he asked the British government to send a representative to Washington to help settle the boundary dispute.

England agreed and sent Lord Ashburton as a special envoy. He began to meet with Secretary of State Webster regularly to try to iron out the difference between the two nations.

One of the main problems facing the two men was the fact that the boundary maps attached to the original peace treaty between the two countries was missing. Lord Ashburton sent word back to London that they should look for the maps there and Webster sent word to Paris, where the treaty was signed, asking them to look for the maps as well.

Both men found maps. The one sent to Webster was marked by Benjamin Franklin and showed the border far into Maine where United States citizens were now living. The one sent to Lord Ashburton was drawn up for King George III and showed the border much further into Canada than Maine was even claiming. Neither man wanted to show the other one his map, but each one was willing to draw the line somewhere in the middle.

When the treaty was signed it marked the first time since the Revolutionary War that relationships between England and America were cordial. It showed that two powerful nations could sit down and work out their differences without going to war.

Although he was doing a masterful job for President Tyler as Secretary of State and the president was very thankful that he had stayed in the cabinet when Clay got all the other Whigs to resign, there was one issue on which they could not agree. Tyler wanted Texas to be admitted to the Union and Daniel did not want another slave state sending congressmen to Washington. When the president continued to push for acceptance of Texas as a state Daniel felt that he had to resign.

Returning to Boston as a private citizen, Daniel soon found he had all the business he could handle as a lawyer. One case he argued before the Supreme Court was particularly important to him because it dealt with religious education. A man by the name of Stephen Girard died and in his will gave money to the city of Philadelphia to start a school for orphans. That was fine. But he went on to require that no minister or missionary would ever be allowed to teach in the school, ''nor shall any such person ever be admitted for any purpose, or as a visitor, within the premises appropriated to the purposes of the said college.''

Some of the heirs of Girard contested the will and Daniel was representing them before the court. He argued that the school could not be considered a charity under the laws of the United States because ''the plan of education proposed by Mr. Girard is derogatory to the Christian religion.'' He pointed out to the court that ''the proposed school is to be founded on plain and clear principles, and for plain and clear objects, of infidelity.''

The reason this kept the school from being a charity was because the will was ''against the public policy of the State of Pennsylvania, in which state Christianity is declared to be the law of the land.''

After stating his case clearly for the judges, Daniel began to show how greatly the Christian religion had affected the growth and development of the nation. He reminded the court of the tremendous influence for good which ministers of the gospel had accomplished, and then asked, ''They are not to be allowed even the ordinary rights of hospitality; not even to be permitted to put their foot over the threshold of this college?''

''I maintain that in any institution for the instruction of youth, where the authority of God is disowned and the duties of Christianity derided and despised, and its ministers shut out from all participation in its proceedings,'' he thundered, ''there can be no more charity, true charity, found to exist, than evil can spring out of the Bible, error out of truth, or hatred and animosity come forth from the bosom of perfect love. No, sir!''

It was obvious to everyone who listened that the matter was very dear to Daniel's heart. As he spoke he thought of the many hours of religious instruction his wife had given to their children. How sad it would be if orphans in a public institution were denied that same training.

''When little children were brought into the presence of the Son of God,'' he said, ''His disciples proposed to send them away, but he said, 'Suffer little children to come unto me.' Unto me; he did not

send them first for lessons in morals to the schools of the Pharisees, or to the unbelieving Sadducees, he opened at once to the youthful mind the everlasting fountain of living waters, the only source of eternal truths: 'Suffer little children to come unto me.' And that injunction is of perpetual obligation. It extends to the ends of the earth, it will reach to the end of time."

Daniel's feelings on the subject of Christian education had never been more clearly stated. The speech was printed and read in churches all across the country. The great defender of the Constitution had demonstrated that the reason his country was great was because of its belief in God.

Secession Averted

As much as Webster loved living at Marshfield and working as a lawyer, people were not content to leave him there. A great storm was gathering over the nation which threatened to destroy the Union Daniel loved so much. Texas was pushing for admission to the Union as a slave state, and many people were saying the country should be extended all the way to the Pacific Ocean. That would certainly mean war with England in the north and Mexico in the south as well as opening up much more area for slavery.

In 1844 the Whigs passed over their own president, John Tyler and nominated Henry Clay to run. The Democrats were split between Calhoun, President Tyler and former President Van Buren, so they didn't nominate any of them. They chose a man very few people had ever heard of by the name of James K. Polk. Everyone thought that there was no way a man no one knew could beat the great Henry Clay, but Clay's supporters didn't want to take any chances. They asked Daniel to travel around the country giving

speeches for them as he had for William Harrison.
Even though Clay had been very unkind to Daniel
he did what he thought would be best for the country
and traveled around speaking to support the candidacy
of Henry Clay.

Clay, however, made a serious mistake. He told
some supporters from the North that he was opposed
to the admission of Texas and he told some southern
Whigs that he didn't really object to statehood for
Texas. When both of those statements were published
people decided that no one could trust Clay. The dark
horse Polk won the election.

Now the Whig Party was without any leadership,
and Daniel was persuaded to return to the Senate in
March of 1845. The new president, James Polk, was
one of those who believed in "Manifest Destiny," that
it was the right of the United States to own the land
all the way to the Pacific Ocean. His campaign slogan
had been "Fifty-four Forty or Fight" meaning that
he would fight with England over land in the
Northwest unless they agreed to a border in the place
Polk wanted it to be.

Daniel was opposed to war as he had been all his
life. He was particularly opposed to war with England
after helping to settle the land dispute in New England
with the Webster-Ashburton Treaty. In fact he had
tried to arrange for a border at the forty-ninth parallel
between the Northwest and Canada at that time but
the British government had not agreed.

As soon as he was back in the Senate Daniel began
to speak against war. He also met with his friends from
England and tried to convince them that the forty-
ninth parallel would be a fair division of the land for
both countires. To his delight they agreed and asked
him to present the idea to President Polk as well.

Daniel said he would, knowing that the president

probably would not like the idea, especially since he had run for president on the promise to fight if they didn't get all the territory they wanted. However, Texas had been admitted to the Union by that time and the Mexican War had started. President Polk didn't want to fight two wars at once so he was glad to settle the matter of the northwest boundary without fighting. Once again Daniel had managed to avoid a war by using his powers of persuasion instead.

The war with Mexico, however, he had not been able to avoid. Now that it was started, he supported the effort in Congress to give the President the money and materials he needed to win. His son Edward raised the first company of volunteers accepted by the state of Massachusetts and went to the front in Mexico at the head of his own regiment.

Soon reports of victory were received in Washington and members of Polk's cabinet began to talk of annexing all of Mexico. Daniel went before the Senate and spoke against such as idea. "We want no extension of territory," he said, "we want no accession of new states. The country is already large enough." Then he went to the very heart of the matter. "Sir, I fear we are not yet arrived at the beginning of the end of controversy. I present to see but little of the future, and that little affords no gratification. All I can scan is contention, strife and agitation. We are suffering to pass the golden opportunity for securing harmony and stability of the Constitution. We appear to me to be rushing upon perils headlong, and with our eyes wide open."

Perhaps better than any other man he saw where the issue of slavery was leading the country and his heart ached for some way to help preserve the Union without a war.

On February 23, 1848, a military dispatch bearer rode into Washington.

"The war is over," he shouted. "A treaty of peace has been signed."

Two weeks earlier a treaty had been signed at Guadalupe Hidalgo which made the Rio Grande the border between Texas and Mexico and also sold the land west of Texas to the United States for fifteen million dollars. But the dispatch bearer carried another message as well. Edward Webster had died of typhoid fever in Mexico City on January 23rd.

Broken-hearted, Daniel hurried back to Boston to break the news to Julia who was also ill. When he got there it was obvious that she, too, was dying of tuberculosis. He buried her on May 1, the same day Edward's body arrived from Mexico.

For the next several days Daniel was sick himself from sorrow and exhaustion. The only thing that cheered him was reading from the Bible. Friends who came by to offer sympathy would find him pacing the floor and reading aloud from the Word of God. His only comfort in the loss of so many he loved was to know that one day he would be reunited with them in heaven.

He had stated this himself in a tribute he gave when his good friend Justice Joseph Story had died three years before. "The bed of death brings every human being to his pure individuality; to the intense contemplation of that deepest and most solemn of all relations, the relation between the creature and his Creator," Webster had said. "Here it is that fame and renown cannot assist us; that all external things must fail to aid us; that even friends, affection and human love and devotedness cannot succor us. This relation, the true foundation of all duty, a relation perceived and felt by conscience and confirmed by revelation, our illustrious friend, now deceased, always acknowledged. He reverenced the Scriptures of truth, honored the pure morality which they teach, and clung to the hopes of future life which they impart. He beheld enough in nature, in himself, and in all that can be known of things seen, to feel assured that there is a Supreme Power, without whose providence not a sparrow falleth to the ground. To this gracious Being he trusted himself for time and for eternity; and the last words of his lips ever heard by mortal ears were a fervent supplication to his Maker to take him to himself."

In spite of his sorrow over the loss of two more of his children, Daniel forced himself to take an interest in the coming election. Henry Clay had been nominated and defeated three times and he was not going to try again, so many of Daniel's friends believed this was the year he would receive the nomination. But the Democrats nominated a soldier named General Cass and the Whigs decided they should do the same. They gave the nomination to General Zachary Taylor, a hero of the Mexican War. Webster tried to tell them that General Taylor had no knowledge of politics, wasn't even a Whig and owned over three hundred slaves, but the convention would not listen. Instead they offered to nominate Daniel for vice president.

Now sixty-six years old and believing his last chance to be president had come and gone, Webster refused.

President Taylor was sworn in on March 5, 1849, and Daniel returned once again to his seat in the Senate. It was obvious to him and to everyone in Washington that slavery was going to bring the nation to a crisis very soon. Oregon had been admitted as a free state to balance the admission of Texas. But now with the gold rush going on, California was asking to be admitted. There was also the land recently purchased from Mexico to consider.

John Calhoun was arguing that land purchased with federal money should be open for slavery. Northern abolitionists wanted slavery excluded from all the new states. Stephen Douglas came up with the idea of "popular sovereignty," that each new state should be allowed to decide for itself what it wanted to do about slavery. Complicating the entire matter was the fact that Mexico had abolished slavery in all of its territory twenty-four years earlier. If the new states allowed slavery they would in effect be turning free soil back into slave soil.

Daniel's position on slavery had always been clear. As early as 1820 he had opposed the Missouri Compromise because it allowed slavery in Missouri. His

Plymouth Oration was still remembered for its vivid description of the "furnaces where manacles and fetters are still being forged for human limbs." In his great Reply to Hayne he opposed slavery vigorously. In debate on the annexation of Texas he had called slavery "a great moral, social and political evil."

Though he was quite old and very weak, Henry Clay introduced what he called the Compromise of 1850 and spoke at length in favor of his idea. The Compromise would admit California as a free state, but would not bar slavery from the rest of the territory purchased from Mexico. The slave trade would be abolished in the District of Columbia, but slavery itself would continue in the capital until Maryland approved ending it. The North would agree not to interfere with slavery in the South and there would be a strong fugitive slave law to return runaway slaves to their owners.

Although Clay tried to include something everyone would like in the Compromise he also included something everyone would hate. John Calhoun, dying of pneumonia, forced himself out of bed and came to the Senate to speak against Clay for the last time. Not even strong enough to read his speech, he sat wrapped in flannel blankets while Senator James Mason of Virginia read it for him. The speech began, "You have forced upon you the greatest and gravest question that can ever come under your consideration: How can the Union be preserved? If the agitation goes on, nothing will be left to hold the states together except force." He was warning that the South would fight if the North did not leave slavery alone. It was Calhoun's last speech in the Senate. He died before the month was over.

Now that Clay had spoken in favor of the Compromise and Calhoun against it, the time had come for Webster to speak. His influence was still so great that it was obvious the Senate would do what he asked them to do. If he joined Calhoun in opposition to the Compromise, though for different reasons, the Compromise would be defeated. If he joined Clay in support for the Compromise, it would be passed.

On the seventh of March, 1850, it was noised abroad in Washington that Webster was going to give a speech. Like that day many years earlier when he had replied to Hayne, the galleries, lobbies and the Senate floor were crowded and overflowing with people. Senator Walker of Wisconsin had started a speech the day before which he had not finished, but seeing the crowd he rose and said, "Mr. President, this vast audience has not come together to hear me, and there is but one man, in my opinion, who can assemble such an audience. They expect to hear him, and I feel it is to be my duty, therefore, as it is my pleasure to give the floor to the Senator from Massachusetts."

Thanking Walker for his gracious spirit, Daniel rose and walked to the front of the room. There he paused and looked out over the crowd until a hush fell across the chamber. "Mr. President," he began. "I wish to speak today, not as a Massachusetts man, nor as a northern man, but as an American, and a member of the Senate of the United States. I speak today for the preservation of the Union."

What Daniel said that day was not what many people expected. He reviewed the history of slavery, making it clear that he was personally opposed to it. He admitted that the Constitution permitted slavery in the South, but reminded the audience that they were not there to discuss what to do about that. They were there to discuss the extension of slavery to new territories acquired from Mexico.

After a lengthy discussion of the background of the

debate, Daniel moved to the matter which was closest
to his heart, the matter he said he would address at
the beginning of his speech. "I hear with distress and
anguish the word 'secession,' especially when it falls
from lips of those who are patriotic, and known all
over the world for their political services. Peaceable
secession. Who is so foolish, I beg everybody's par-
don, as to expect to see any such thing? There is no
such thing as a peaceable secession."

Clay and Calhoun, Jefferson Davis and Sam
Houston, Stephen Douglas and Lewis Cass, along
with every other person in the room stared as Webster
roared in the most powerful words they had ever heard
his feeling for the Union. "What would be the result?
Where is the line to be drawn? What States are to
secede? What is to remain American? What am I to
be? An American no longer? Am I to become a sec-
tional man, a local man, a separatist, with no country
in common with the gentlemen who sit around me
here, or who fill the other house of Congress? Heaven
forbid! Where is the flag of the republic to remain?
Where is the eagle yet to tower? Or is he to cower,

and shrink, and fall to the ground? How is each of the thirty States to defend itself? To break up this great government! To dismember this glorious country! to astonish Europe with an act of folly such as Europe for two centuries has never beheld in any government or any people! No sir! No sir! There will be no secession!''

To the astonishment of his friends from the North, Daniel then supported Clay's Compromise bill. ''Let our understanding be as broad as the country for which we act,'' he appealed to them.

With Webster's support the bill passed and the secession of the southern states was averted. Although it cost him many friends, Daniel had once again preserved his precious Union. As much as he was personally opposed to slavery he knew that secession was impossible without conflict. He believed, as he had all his life, that political differences could be solved without war.

We the People...

17

Last Years of the Defender of the Constitution

The results of Daniel's speech in support of the Compromise of 1850 were not immediately known. Many people did not realize that he had preserved the Union. Instead they believed he had betrayed the North and the cause of those who opposed slavery. Theodore Parker, in a meeting at Faneuil Hall in Boston, compared what Webster had done to the treachery of Benedict Arnold. Remembering how his father had been trusted by George Washington on that occasion, Daniel was terribly hurt by that charge.

Horace Mann called him a "fallen star, Lucifer descending from heaven." John Greenleaf Whittier wrote a poem called "Ichabod" in which he described Daniel's loss of faith and honor."

One of the main reasons his friends were so upset by the speech was because they did not believe the South would ever carry out their threats to secede. They did not think the Union was in any danger. It was not until the War between the States began ten years later that they would understand what Daniel had done.

Some, however, appreciated the stand Daniel took. A young lawyer from Illinois by the name of Abraham Lincoln read the speech and was greatly influenced by it. He would use many of Daniel's ideas in speeches he gave when he became president.

Because of all the criticism, especially from New England, Daniel seriously considered leaving the Senate. Once again he had taken a strong stand only to be misunderstood. He was not sorry about what he had done. When the adoption of the Compromise was assured, he said "we have gone through the most important crisis which has occurred since the foundation of the government; and whatever party may prevail, hereafter, the Union stands firm. Faction, disunion, and the love of mischief are put under, at least for the present, and I hope for a long time."

Then an event took place which made it possible for him to resign and still remain active in public life.

On the fourth of July 1850, there was a great celebration in Washington. A new memorial was to be built to honor George Washington and on that day

President Taylor laid the cornerstone for the great Washington Monument. During the ceremony the President became sick and five days later died of cholera. Had Webster been willing to accept second place to Taylor as vice president he would have attained his goal to become chief executive. Instead Millard Fillmore became the president and asked Webster to be his Secretary of State.

Once again Daniel moved to the familiar desk in the Secretary of State's office. Away from the controversy of Congress he enjoyed his work with the State Department. He rose early each morning for an hour of fishing and then spent ten to twelve hours at his desk.

During this second period of time as Secretary of State Webster sent Matthew Perry to Japan to open that country to trade with the western world by making a commercial treaty with the emperor. He also dealt with problems in the nation's relations with Austria, Spain, England and Mexico.

When the election of 1852 drew near there was once more a movement to nominate Daniel for president. The only real issue facing the country was slavery, but after the Compromise of 1850 people both in the North and the South were trying to convince the country that the slavery issue no longer existed. Because of his speech in support of the Union many felt Daniel would get the nomination. He was willing to run. "It is a great office and I want it," he wrote to a friend.

The Democratic convention met first and nominated General Franklin Pierce of New Hampshire, a man Daniel had known as a boy. The Whigs met two weeks later to try to decide between President Fillmore who had replaced Zachary Taylor, General Winfield Scott, another hero of the Mexican War, and Daniel Webster. The southern Whigs, who appreciated Daniel's support of the Compromise, were promised to President Fillmore. The northern Whigs, who felt Daniel had betrayed them, were in favor of General Scott. When the convention finally nominated the general on the fifty-third ballot Daniel remarked, "It was not my good fortune to be a successful military chieftain."

Henry Clay, who was not considered for nomination that year, died soon after the convention.

Daniel refused to campaign for General Scott. Instead he urged his friends to vote for Franklin Pierce who was committed to upholding the Compromise of 1850.

Late in July, 1852, Daniel left Washington for the last time to return to Marshfield. When his train stopped at Kingston, nine miles from his home, he was surprised to find a large crowd of neighbors waiting at the station. Pleased with their reception he invited them to Marshfield. There he spoke briefly, thanking them for their friendship. It was his last speech.

For three months Daniel battled illness. Finally in October he was confined to his bed. Dr. Jeffries came to see him.

"I would like to you send for Dr. Mason Warren to be with me in the end, Doctor. I don't believe I will make it through another night."

Caroline and his only remaining son Daniel Fletcher, called the household staff together along with some close friends. Daniel signed his will and then raised himself slightly off the bed. Speaking in a voice which because of his illness was only a shadow of its former self, he talked about God. He told how ever since childhood he had believed in the existence of God and the necessity of trusting in Him for the hope of immortality. Then he turned to Dr. Warren.

"Tell us, Dr. Warren, Tell all of us what will happen to one who trusts in God at the moment of death. Then read the Twenty-third Psalm."

As the minister read the familiar psalm, those gathered around the bed heard Daniel whisper, "Yes, Thy rod, Thy staff—but the fact, the fact I want."

Early the next morning, Webster woke and called out, "I still live," and then turned over in his bed and died.

The entire nation mourned for the man who had stood for the Union. Great men eulogized him and presidents and politicians gave him honor. But the remark Daniel would have liked best was made by one of his neighbors as he passed by the coffin.

"Daniel Webster," said the farmer. "The world without you will be lonesome."

CHRONOLOGY

1782   Born January 18 in Salisbury, New Hampshire.

1789   George Washington is inaugurated as the first President of the United States.

1796   Becomes a student at Phillips Exeter Academy.

1797   Enrolls at Dartmouth College.

1800   Delivers the Fourth of July Oration in Hanover, New Hampshire.

1801   Graduates from Dartmouth.

1802   Teaches school in Fryeburg, Maine.

1804   Becomes a clerk in the office of Christopher Gore in Boston.

1805   Admitted to the Massachusetts Bar.

1808   Marries Miss Grace Fletcher.

1812   Elected from the Portsmouth district to a seat in the Congress of the United States.

1816   Moves from Portsmouth to Boston.

1818   Argues the Dartmouth College case before the Supreme Court.

1820   Delivers the Plymouth Oration to commemorate the coming of the Pilgrims.

1822   Elected by the Suffolk, Massachusetts, district to Congress.

1826   Presidents Adams and Jefferson die on July 4. Delivers eulogy on August 2.

1827   Elected to the United States Senate.

1828   Mrs Grace Webster dies.

1829   His brother Ezekiel dies. Marries Caroline LeRoy.

1830   Delivers his "Reply to Hayne" during debate on the nature of the Union.

1833   Delivers "The Constitution not a Compact
        between Soverign States," in reply to
        Calhoun.
1835   Nominated   for   president   by   the
        Massachusetts legislature.
1836   Martin Van Buren is elected President.
1837   Delivers speech at Niblo's Garden in New
        York.
1839   Visits Great Britain and Europe.
1840   William   Henry   Harrison   is   elected
        President, dies and is succeeded by John
        Tyler who asks him to become Secretary
        of State.
1841   Resigns from the Senate.
1842   Signs the Webster-Ashburton Treaty.
1843   Resigns as Secretary of State.
1844   Supports Henry Clay for President. James
        K. Polk is elected.
1848   Edward and Julia die. General Zachary
        Taylor is elected President.
1850   Delivers his "Seventh of March" speech   in
        favor of the Compromise of 1850. President
        Taylor dies and is succeeded by Millard
        Fillmore who asks him to become Secretary
        of State.
1852   Dies October 24 at his home near Boston.

BIBLIOGRAPHY

Bartlett, Irving H. *Daniel Webster*. New York: W. W. Norton and Co., 1978.

Bradford, Gamaliel. *As God Made Them*. Boston: Houghton Mifflin, 1929.

Copeland, Lewis. *The World's Great Speeches*. Garden City: Garden City Pub., 1949.

Current, Richard. *Daniel Webster and the Rise of National Conservatism*. Boston: Little, Brown and Co., 1955.

Dalzell, Robert F. *Daniel Webster and the Trial of American Nationalism*. Boston: Houghton Mifflin, 1973.

Hurd, Charles. *Treasury of Great American Speeches*. New York: Hawthorne, 1959.

Jenkins, Everett, Sargent and Greeley. *Makers of American History*. New York: The University Society, 1905.

Johnson, Gerald W. *America's Silver Age*. New York: Harper, 1939.

Lengyel, Cornel. *I, Benedict Arnold*. Garden City: Doubleday and Co., 1960.

Linton, Calvin D. *The Bicentennial Almanac*. Nashville: Thomas Nelson, 1975.

Lodge, Henry Cabot. *Daniel Webster*. Boston: Houghton Mifflin, 1894.

Lutzweiler, James. *The Olney Hymns of William Cowper*. Minneapolis: Central Seminary, 1972.

McMaster, John. *Daniel Webster*. New York: The Century Co., 1902.

Ogg, Frederic A. *Daniel Webster*. Philadelphia: George W. Jacobs and Co., 1914.

Oliver, Robert T. *History of Public Speaking in America.*
    Boston: Allyn and Bacon, 1965.
Steinburg, Alfred. *Daniel Webster.* New York: G. P.
    Putnam's Sons, 1959.
Webster, Caroline LeRoy. *Mr. W. and I.*
    Binghamton: Washburn, 1942.
Whipple, Edwin P. *Webster's Great Speeches.* Boston:
    Little, Brown and Co., 1899.

INDEX

ABOUT THE AUTHOR

Robert Allen is the father of four children, Chad, Wendy, Kent and Tammy, who love to read his books and listen to his stories. Father and children together have produced a weekly radio program and children's tapes on which they are known as the Bible Story Family. Allen's retelling of the stories of great Old Testament kings has made him a popular speaker at Christian schools and summer camps. He also is known for his monodramas of great American speakers.

Mr. Allen heads the Speech Department at Pillsbury College in Owatonna, Minnesota, where he lives with his wife and family. There he seeks to train others who will help lead the nation through their speaking ability, as Daniel Webster did.

ABOUT THE ARTIST

Michael L. Denman says he has always liked to draw. He remembers that in his poor family paper was scarce. So his grandmother gave him her Christmas cards, which in those days were always folded into fourths. Michael unfolded them and was delighted to have full sheets of paper, blank on one side, ready for his drawings. His favorite books as a child were those on American history and world history, so he especially likes to illustrate history books for today's children. While he was researching for his work on this book, he became so interested in reading about Daniel Webster that he almost forgot to look for the pictures he needed.

Mr. Denman at first learned most of his art skills by himself, but later he studied art at Cooper Institute. For more than ten years he has illustrated children's storybooks, workbooks and readers, as well as visual aids that teachers use. He is an Art Director at McCallum Design Company and lives with his wife and family in North Ridgeville, Ohio.

SOWERS SERIES

Abigail Adams by Evelyn Witter

Johnny Appleseed by David Collins

Robert Boyle by John Hudson Tiner

William Jennings Bryan by Robert Allen

George Washington Carver by David Collins

Christopher Columbus by Bennie Rhodes

George Frideric Handel by Charles Ludwig

Mahalia Jackson by Evelyn Witter

Stonewall Jackson by Charles Ludwig

Johannes Kepler by John Hudson Tiner

Francis Scott Key by David Collins

Jason Lee by Charles Ludwig

Robert E. Lee by Lee Roddy

Abraham Lincoln by David Collins

Samuel F.B. Morse by John Hudson Tiner

Isaac Newton by John Hudson Tiner

Florence Nightingale by David Collins

Louis Pasteur by John Hudson Tiner

Samuel Francis Smith by Marguerite Fitch

Billy Sunday by Robert Allen

Teresa of Calcutta by Jeanene Watson

George Washington by Norma Cournow Camp

Daniel Webster by Robert Allen

Noah Webster by David Collins

Susanna Wesley by Charles Ludwig

The Wright Brothers by Charles Ludwig